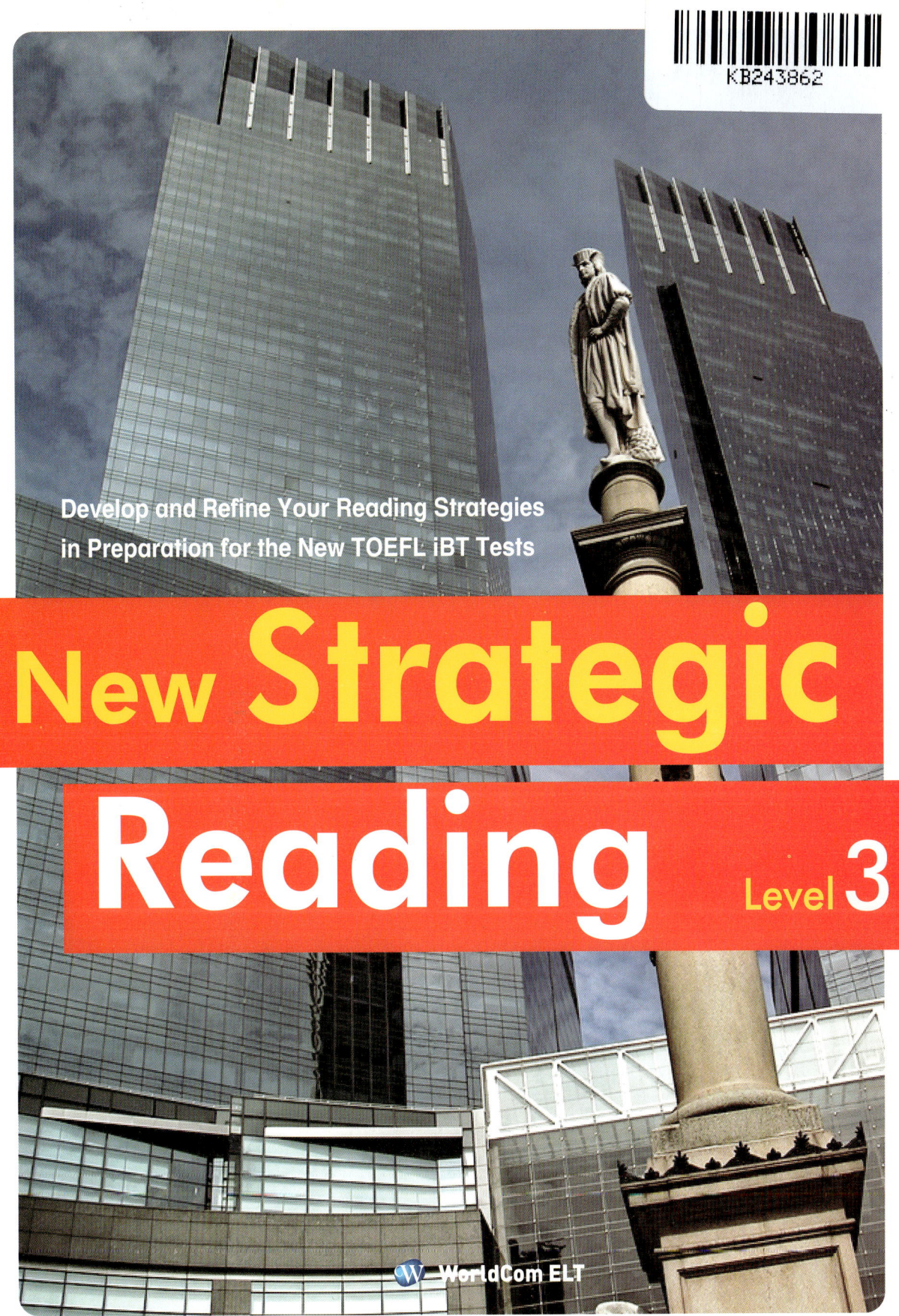

Develop and Refine Your Reading Strategies
in Preparation for the New TOEFL iBT Tests

New Strategic
Reading
Level 3

W WorldCom ELT

New **Strategic** Reading Level **3**

Alice Wrigglesworth & Jonathan Wrigglesworth

ⓒ 2007 published by WorldCom Publishing Inc.

Cover/Interior Design : Joo Design

ISBN : 978-89-90545-63-3

Desk Copy Request / Information
To place your desk copy request or for more information, please contact the following office:
Tel : (02)3273-4300   Fax : (02)3273-4303
Homepage : www.wcbooks.co.kr

Contents

The History of Flight

Pre-reading activity

1. Who was the first person to fly?
2. What was the first flying machine?
3. Who invented the airplane?

1 Since the beginning of human history, people have dreamed of flying. Ancient legends are full of stories of people who flew like birds. Icarus flew to the sun on wings made of wax and Alexander the Great tied four **mythical griffins** to his throne and flew around his realm. These stories show the fascination people have always had for the possibility of flight. Philosophers believed that people could fly by mimicking the flapping wings of birds or floating with gasses that are lighter than air such as smoke. History is full of people who dreamed of making a flying machine. Although most of these attempts failed, over centuries progress was made, until today people can fly anywhere they want.

2 The first aircraft was the **kite** developed around the fifth **century**. The earliest known kites were made in China around 400 BC. These kites were used in religious ceremonies and to test weather conditions. Kites were an important innovation because they opened the possibility of human flight and were the forerunners of balloons and gliders. In the 15th century, Leonardo da Vinci made the first scientific studies of flight. He made over one hundred drawings illustrating his theories of flight. His inventions were doomed to failure during his lifetime because he had no other power source other than the human body, but several of his ideas achieved success in later centuries. He conceived of the first parachute, an airscrew that would be the inspiration for the modern **propeller**, an early version of the helicopter, and a fixed-wing glider. Although he never got off the ground, Leonardo da Vinci was one of the great pioneers of flight.

---

mythical existing in only traditional stories or myths

griffin a mythical creature with the head of an eagle and the body of a lion

century a time period of 100 years

kite a light frame covered with a thin material that is meant to flown in the wind at the end of a loose string

propeller a device that rotates to propel an airplane, ship, etc.

3 It would be over two hundred years before any significant advancement toward flight was made. The year 1783 saw the first hot air balloon flight. Brothers Joseph and Jacques Montgolfier began experimenting with hot air from a fire to fill a silk bag. They tied a huge silk bag to a basket and filled the bag with hot air from a fire; the hot air rose and made the balloon and basket lighter than air. The first passengers in the Montgolfier's balloon were a sheep, a duck, and a rooster. The balloon climbed to a height of about 6,000 feet and traveled over a mile. The first **manned** flight was piloted by Jean-Francois Pilatre de Rozier and Francois Laurent on November 21, 1783.

4 Balloon flight became commonplace over the next century, but because of the lack of control that the pilots had, it had little practical use. George Cayley began to experiment with a design that would allow manned controlled flight. His work resulted in the first manned glider flights. In over fifty years of experiments, he developed a wing design that allowed air to flow efficiently over the wings and a tail for stability. He wrote that a fixed wing design was the best hope for manned controlled flight; he also recognized that a power source would be needed to achieve this.

5 In 1891, Samuel P. Langley successfully combined a fixed-wing glider design with a power source — a steam powered engine. He called his design the aerodrome. His model aerodrome successfully flew for three quarters of a mile before running out of fuel. He received a grant of $50,000 to build a full-size aerodrome. His prototype proved to be too heavy and crashed. Langley became discouraged and never tried to fly again.

6 Although Langley failed in his efforts to fly, the idea of a fixed-wing glider with a power source would ultimately prove to be successful. Brothers Orville and Wilbur Wright meticulously studied all of the previous attempts at flight. They read everything that had been written on the subject and did experiments to determine the best design for a glider. Finally, they added a power source — a 12 horsepower gas engine. Their invention weighed six hundred and five pounds. At Kitty Hawk, North Carolina, U.S.A., the first heavier-than-air manned flight took place. Orville flew for only 12 seconds and traveled 120 feet, but a controlled, manned heavier-than-air flight had been achieved.

....

manned carrying or operated by a person

Vocabulary Study I

Match the word with its synonym.

1. realm   a. blueprint
2. ceremony   b. commemoration
3. innovation   c. model
4. design   d. change
5. prototype   e. area

Reading comprehension I

Main idea

What's the passage about?

a. The first hot air balloon   b. The Wright brothers

c. Leonardo da Vinci   d. The history of flight

Detail questions

1. The first kites were made in

    a. China   b. Japan

    c. England   d. France

2. The first hot air balloon was made by _____.

    a. the Wright brothers   b. George Cayley

    c. Leonardo da Vinci   d. the Montgolfier brothers

3. Leonardo da Vinci's flying machines couldn't work during his lifetime because

    _____.

    a. he didn't have the right materials   b. his ideas were wrong

    c. he didn't have a power source   d. flying was against the law

Word root: mand, mend

1. **command** = com (with) + mand (order)
   demand = de (away) + mand (order)
   countermand = counter (against) + mand (order)

2. **command:** with, order → to require an action
   demand: away, order → to ask with authority
   countermand: against, order → to revoke an order

3. Complete the following sentences choosing the right word.

   > commanded   demanded   countermanded

   a. The general _____ the sergeant's order.

   b. I _____ a clean plate in the restaurant.

   c. The general _____ his troops.

Reading comprehension II

Inference and purpose

It can be inferred from the passage that _____ .

   a. the Wright brothers stole Leonardo da Vinci's ideas
   b. Leonardo da Vinci was the first person to fly a glider
   c. there have been great advances in the design of airplanes
   d. the Wright brothers flew around the world

Coherence

Look at the four squares [■] that indicate where the following sentence can be added to the passage below. Where would the sentence best fit?

Balloons were primarily used by the rich for recreational purposes.

■ Balloon flight became commonplace over the next century, but because of the lack of control that the pilots had it had little practical use. ■ George Cayley began to experiment with a design that would allow manned controlled flight. ■ His work resulted in the first manned glider flights. In over fifty years of experiments, he developed a wing design that allowed air to flow efficiently over the wings and a tail for stability. ■

Listening comprehension

Main idea

What is the lecture mainly about?

    a. The first air balloon flight

    b. A brief history of Europe

    c. Jean-Francois Pilatre de Rozier

    d. Advances in flight

Details

1. What is true about the first air balloon flight?

    a. The bag was not filled with hot air.

    b. It was made in 1873.

    c. Brothers Joseph and Jacques Montgolfier tried it.

    d. No roosters boarded the Montgolfier's balloon.

2. What is true about the first manned flight?

    a. Jean-Francois Pilatre de Rozier and Francois Laurent piloted it.

    b. A sheep accompanied the flight.

    c. It covered only one mile.

    d. It was made on November 31, 1783.

Paraphrasing

It would be over two hundred years before any significant advancement toward flight was made.

Which of the sentences below best expresses the essential information in the highlighted sentence in the passage? Incorrect choices change the meaning in important ways or leave out essential information.

    a. Over the next two hundred years many advancements in flight were made.

    b. After two hundred years of little advancement, some significant advancements were made in flight

    c. Over two hundred significant advancements were made in flight.

    d. For over two hundred years many advancements were made in flight.

Summary

Complete the following list by choosing the three true sentences about the passage.

-
-
-

a. Orville Wright was the first person to fly in a heavier-than-air powered machine.
b. The first kites were made in America.
c. Wilbur Wright was the first person to fly in a glider.
d. The Montgolfier brothers made the first hot air balloon.
e. Leonardo da Vinci flew in a helicopter.
f. A sheep, a duck, and a rooster were the first animals to fly in a hot air balloon.

Speaking

What is the most important invention to you?

Model response

1. Fill in the blanks using the words in the box.

invention	communicate	everything	talk	questions	plans

The most important _____ to me is the Internet. I can do _____ on the Internet. I use the Internet to _____ to friends, to do my homework, and to play games. My friends and I all use the Internet to _____ with each other. We can email or use instant messages to talk to each other. This is a great way for us to make _____ or to just have fun. The Internet is also very useful when I do my homework. There are even places on the Internet where I can go and have a teacher answer my _____. This is great especially when I don't know the answer. The thing I like to do the most on the Internet is to play games. There are always new games available and they are a lot of fun.

2. Using your own words, answer the question above. Then talk to the class.

Mozart

Pre-reading activity

1. What is your favorite type of music?
2. Have you ever tried to write music?
3. Have you heard of Amadeus Mozart?

1 Imagine what your life would be like if you were a superstar singer or sports star. Now imagine that you were a superstar at age five. That is what the childhood of Amadeus Mozart was like. Mozart was born in Salzburg, **Austria**, in 1756. His father, Leopold, a successful composer and musician, introduced the young Mozart to the world of music and composing at an early age. It didn't take long for Leopold to realize that his son had a special talent. By age five, Amadeus was composing music as well as the most talented adults of the day. He went on to become one of the most creative composers of all time and one of the most important figures in European classical music.

2 When Amadeus was just a child, he and his father and older sister, Anna, toured the royal courts of Europe. Leopold devoted much of his time to his talented children. Although Anna was gifted, Amadeus's talent was truly remarkable. As a child, he could listen to a piece of music once and then play it perfectly from memory. He could also play the **keyboard** and violin blindfolded. As Amadeus grew older, his reputation also grew. He made a living selling his compositions, giving **concerts**, and teaching music lessons to wealthy families. Although he was successful, he had a taste for an expensive lifestyle. He enjoyed fancy clothes and lavish parties. As a result, he was frequently in debt.

Austria a country located in central Europe
keyboard piano

concert a musical performance in front of an audience

3 Mozart never had a strong work ethic. He would often take a commission for a piece of music and then wait until the last minute before beginning to work on it. One of his most famous works is "Don Giovanni." Although he had months to work on the score, he waited until the night before it was to be performed before writing it. This is a testament to the genius of Mozart. Not only could he create works superior to other composers, he did it seemingly without trying. Many of his works, such as "The Magic Flute," "The Marriage of Figaro," and "Don Giovanni" are still among the most frequently played pieces of classical music played today.

4 Mozart had always been in fragile health but in the spring of 1791 he became seriously ill. His condition worsened until his death on December 5th, 1791. The cause of his illness has been a source of much disagreement among scholars. The theories range from **trichinosis** and influenza to mercury poison. There are some who believe that Mozart was murdered by a fellow composer who was jealous of his talent. Appropriately, his final work was a **requiem**. Many people think that he was thinking of his own **impending** death as he worked on this moving piece. Mozart died at age 35 before he could finish his final work.

---

trichinosis a disease caused by eating undercooked meat especially pork

requiem a song written to be performed at a memorial to a dead person

impending soon to happen, imminent

Vocabulary Study I

Match the word with its synonym.

1. superstar
2. compose
3. talent
4. special
5. ethic

a. unique
b. belief
c. create
d. celebrity
e. ability

Reading comprehension I

Main idea

What's the passage about?

a. Classical music
c. The Mozart family

b. Amadeus Mozart
d. Salzburg, Austria

Detail questions

1. Amadeus Mozart was born in _____.

a. Berlin
c. Salzburg

b. London
d. Rome

2. One of Mozart's most famous works is _____.

a. Don Juan
c. Don Giovanni

b. Don the Barber
d. Don Figaro

3. Mozart made a living _____.

a. teaching music
c. giving concerts

b. selling his compositions
d. all of the above

Vocabulary Study II

Word root: dext

1. **ambidextrous** = ambi (both) + dext (skillful) + (e)r (one who) + ous (possesses quality)

   dexterity = dext (skillful) + er (one who) + ity (forms nouns)

   dexterous = dext (skillful) + er (one who) + ous (possesses quality)

2. **ambidextrous:** both, skillful, person, has quality → skillful with both hands

   dexterity: skillful, person, noun → agility or skill with body

   dexterous: skillful, person, has quality → agility or skill with body

3. Complete the following sentences choosing the right word.

   > ambidextrous   dexterity   dexterous

   a. His _____ made him good at card tricks.

   b. An _____ person can write with either hand.

   c. The piano piece allowed him to show his _____ playing.

Reading comprehension II

Inference and purpose

It can be inferred from the passage that _____.

   a. Mozart is still famous

   b. Leopold was a better composer than Amadeus

   c. Anna was the most talented of the Mozart family

   d. Amadeus's mother hated music

Coherence

Look at the four squares [■] that indicate where the following sentence can be added to the passage below. Where would the sentence best fit?

> **This created jealousy and admiration among his peers.**

■ Mozart never had a strong work ethic. ■ He would often take a commission for a piece of music and then wait until the last minute before beginning to work on it. One of his most famous works is "Don Giovanni." Although he had months to work on the score, he waited until the night before it was to be performed before writing it. This is a testament to the genius of Mozart. Not only could he create works superior to other composers, he did it seemingly without trying. ■ Many of his works, such as "The Magic flute," "The Marriage of Figaro," and Don Giovanni" are still among the most frequently played pieces of classical music played today. ■

Listening comprehension

Main idea

What is the lecture mainly about?

    a. Palaces of Europe
    b. Anna's tragic life

    c. Amadeus's talent and his life
    d. Amadeus's simple life

Details

1. What is true about Anna?

    a. She lived a tragic life.

    b. She had a talent for music.

    c. She was a very wealthy woman.

    d. She was Amadeus's wife.

2. What is true about Amadeus?

    a. He was very popular.

    b. He couldn't play the violin.

    c. He had no talent for music.

    d. He gave no concerts.

Paraphrasing

Leopold devoted much of his time to his talented children.

Which of the sentences below best expresses the essential information in the highlighted sentence in the passage? Incorrect choices change the meaning in important ways or leave out essential information.

    a. Leopold devoted his time to developing talent in his children.

    b. His talented children were devoted to Leopold.

    c. A great deal of Leopold's waking hours were spent on his gifted offspring.

    d. Leopold didn't have much time for his talented children.

Summary

Complete the following list by choosing the three true sentences about the passage.

-
-
-

a. Amadeus was born in Salzburg.

b. Amadeus died of influenza.

c. Amadeus loved fancy clothes.

d. Amadeus Mozart died a sudden death.

e. Leopold Mozart was a music composer.

f. Anna Mozart couldn't play music.

Speaking

How do you feel when you listen to music?

Model response

1. Fill in the blanks using the words in the box.

> energy   lyrics   emotions   sad   friends   listen

Music can make me feel many different _____. Some songs have very sad _____; these songs remind me of times when I felt _____. Other songs have an upbeat tempo; these songs can give me a lot of _____ and make me want to dance. I love to _____ to this type of music when I'm with my _____. Often what music I listen to depends on my mood.

2. Using your own words, answer the question above. Then talk to the class.

Light Pollution

Pre-reading activity
1. Do you turn off the lights when you leave a room?
2. Can a city have too many lights?
3. Have you ever heard of light pollution?

1 Every year the world is becoming more and more aware of the damage pollution is doing to our environment. Stories about air and water pollution and the damage they do to the environment and ecosystems are frequently in the news, but there is another type of pollution that isn't as well reported. Light is a **byproduct** of an industrialized society, so as many countries have become more industrialized, cities have grown and so has the amount of light they give off. The main sources of light pollution include interior lighting, advertising, offices, factories, streetlights, and sporting stadiums. In some parts of the world, especially North America, Europe, and Japan, light pollution has become a source of concern for many people.

2 Beginning in the early 1980's, the "dark-sky movement" emerged as people became concerned about the amount of light pollution. The movement began with amateur and professional astronomers who were **alarmed** that the amount of unnatural light from **urban** areas was making it difficult to see many stars. Light pollution has become so severe that the Griffith Observatory— one of the most famous observatories in America — has become useless for observing the night sky, and the world-famous Palomar Observatory near San Diego is now threatened by the city lights. With technology advancing to make private spaceflight possible, some people are concerned that giant billboards might be placed in space.

byproduct a secondary, usually useless product that can sometimes be harmful

alarmed experiencing a sudden sense of danger
urban relating to a city or town

3 Astronomers aren't the only people who are concerned about light pollution; it has been shown to waste energy, harm human health, and disrupt ecosystems. When the night sky is light, this is a sign of wasted energy. Studies have shown that lighting is one fourth of all energy used worldwide. Wasted light is a huge source of lost resources. In addition, doctors have associated excessive exposure to light with increased incidence of headaches, fatigue, stress, anxiety, and breast cancer.

4 While people are able to adjust to nighttime light by using curtains or other means, animals have to function in the light or dark as it is. Life on Earth evolved with a natural pattern of light and dark; in many areas this natural pattern has been disrupted. Light pollution can confuse animals' navigation, change competition between animal species, and alter animal physiology. For example, city lights can disorient migrating birds. The US Fish and Wildlife Service estimates that 4 ~ 5 million birds are killed after being attracted to lighted city buildings. Also, some nocturnal animals such as some frogs and salamanders only wake when there is no light. When the ecosystem is disrupted by light pollution, these animals may have limited waking hours, giving them less time to find food and reproduce.

5 Advocates for the reduction of light pollution offer many suggestions for reducing the amount of unnecessary light: using the minimum amount of light necessary for the **task**, turning lights off when not in use, improving lighting **fixtures** so they direct the light where it is needed, and adjusting lighting plans to eliminate lighting where it isn't needed. As more people become aware of the **hazards** of light pollution, perhaps these suggestions will be put into practice.

....

task a piece of work or assignment
fixture something permanently attached to a
     house, apartment, building, etc.

hazard something causing unavoidable danger

Vocabulary Study I

Match the word with its synonym.

1. pollution	a. group of living things
2. environment	b. basis
3. ecosystem	c. surroundings
4. source	d. confuse
5. disrupt	e. contamination

Reading comprehension I

Main idea

What's the passage about?

a. Migrating birds   b. Light pollution

c. Types of light   d. Pollution

Detail questions

1. Light pollution is _____ .

   a. the result of the Sun

   b. the result of an industrialized society

   c. a big problem during the day

   d. beneficial to the environment

2. The "dark sky movement" was started by _____ .

   a. night watchmen   b. environmentalists

   c. astronomers   d. biologists

3. The US Fish and Wildlife Service estimates that _____ birds are killed after being attracted to lighted city buildings.

   a. 4 to 5 million   b. 4 to 5 hundred

   c. 5 to 6 million   d. 3 to 4 million

Vocabulary Study II

Word root: fix

1. **suffix =** suf (upon) + fix (attach)
    prefix = pre (before) + fix (attach)
    fixture= fix (attach) + ture (makes a noun)

2. **suffix:** upon, attach → something added to the end of a word
    prefix: before, attach → something added to the beginning of a word
    fixture: attach, noun → something permanently attached

3. Complete the following sentences choosing the right word.

suffix	prefix	fixtures

    a. The house has beautiful light _____ .
    b. The _____ "pre" means before.
    c. The _____ "less" means without.

Reading comprehension II

Inference and purpose

It can be inferred from the passage that _____ .

    a. light pollution is a problem everywhere
    b. light pollution is a problem in Antarctica
    c. light pollution is a problem in New York
    d. light pollution is not a problem anymore

Coherence

Look at the four squares [■] that indicate where the following sentence can be added to the passage below. Where would the sentence best fit?

During this period, the amount of unnecessary light grew in many parts of the world.

■ Beginning in the early 1980's the "dark-sky movement" emerged as people became concerned about the amount of light pollution. ■ The movement began with amateur and professional astronomers who were alarmed that the amount of unnatural light from urban areas was making it difficult to see many stars. ■ Light pollution has become so severe that the Griffith Observatory — one of the most famous observatories in America — has become useless for observing the night sky, and the world famous Palomar Observatory near San Diego is now threatened by the city lights. ■

Listening comprehension

Main idea

What is the lecture mainly about?

    a. Excessive exposure to light

    b. The disruption of ecosystems

    c. The dangers of light pollution

    d. The beauty of the night sky

Details

1. What is true about astronomers?

    a. They waste a lot of energy.

    b. They treat patients.

    c. They are responsible for increased headaches.

    d. They are concerned about light pollution.

2. What is true about increased fatigue?

    a. It is closely related to water pollution.

    b. It is closely related to the moon.

    c. It is associated with excessive exposure to light

    d. It is associated with excessive exposure to loud music.

Paraphrasing

In some parts of the world, especially North America, Europe, and Japan, light pollution has become a source of concern for many people.

Which of the sentences below best expresses the essential information in the highlighted sentence in the passage? Incorrect choices change the meaning in important ways or leave out essential information.

    a. Light pollution has become a reason for worry in many areas, especially North America, Europe, and Japan.

    b. Japan has more light pollution than North America or Europe.

    c. Light pollution is a cause of concern in parts of the world except North America, Europe, and Japan

    d. Light pollution from North America, Europe, and Japan travels around the world.

Summary

Complete the following list by choosing the three true sentences about the passage.

-
-
-

a. One benefit of light pollution is that it improves the functioning of observatories.

b. Light pollution is most severe in South America.

c. Light pollution is a problem in Japan.

d. The first people to become concerned about light pollution were astronomers.

e. Light pollution is the result of excessive farming.

f. Light pollution disrupts some animals' navigation.

Speaking

What annoys you the most?

Model response

1. Fill in the blanks using the words in the box.

> others   enjoy   annoys   someone   whisper   rude

The thing that _____ me the most is people who make noise in the movie theater. When I go to the movies, I like to really _____ the show. I've paid to be there, so I don't want to listen to _____ talking behind me or hear cell phones ringing. I think it is very _____ to make noise in the theater. If you need to talk, you should _____ or go outside. I wish everyone would be considerate of _____.

2. Using your own words, answer the question above. Then talk to the class.

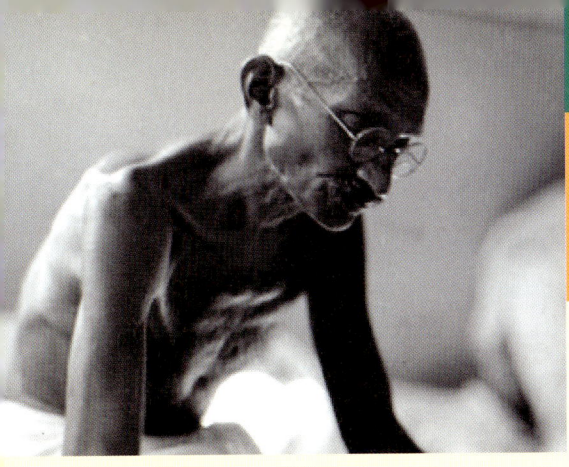

Gandhi

Pre-reading activity
1. What do you know about India?
2. Do you know what passive resistance is?
3. Do you know who Mahatma Gandhi is?

1   Mahatma Gandhi was unimpressive to look at. He was small and frail, but through his passionate, tireless struggle for justice, he made the whole world take notice as he fought for independence for his country. In his native **India** he is sometimes referred to as "the teacher of his nation" or as "the father of his nation." Both of these **titles** seem appropriate.

2   Gandhi was born into a privileged family on October 2, 1869, in India. His upbringing was orthodox Hindu. From an early age, he learned the practices of non-injury to living things, **vegetarianism**, and **fasting**. He was married to Kasturba at age thirteen in an arranged marriage. In his youth, Gandhi was a mediocre student barely passing his college entrance examinations. At the age of 18, he was sent by his family to study law at University College, **London**. Before leaving for London, he made a vow to his mother that he would continue to observe Hindu practices.

3   While in London, he frequented a vegetarian restaurant where he met members of the Theosophical Society. This group was devoted to the promotion of universal brotherhood. With their encouragement, Gandhi read the works of all the major religions of the world. After completing his studies, he returned to India and set up a law practice. He tried his hand at several ventures but was largely unsuccessful. In a fateful move, he accepted a year-long contract from an Indian firm in **South Africa**. It was here that his life's work would begin.

4   While in South Africa, he faced brutal discrimination that was commonly directed at Blacks and Indians. During a train trip he was forced to move to a third class car despite having a valid first class ticket. Later in the trip, he was beaten by a driver for refusing to ride on the footboard to make room for a

India   a country lying south of China and east of Pakistan

title   that by which one is known

vegetarianism   the habit of not eating animal products

European passenger. He was also barred from many hotels. Incidents like these were the turning-point in his life. After witnessing racism, prejudice, and injustice first-hand, Gandhi dedicated his life to social activism.

5 Gandhi had completed his year-long contract and was preparing to return to India. He was attending a good-bye party held in his honor when he learned that legislation was being considered that would deny Indians the right to vote. He abandoned his plans to return to India; instead he stayed in South Africa and fought for Indian rights. He was unsuccessful in stopping the voting ban law, but he was able to bring attention to the injustices that Indians faced in South Africa. Through his political activism, he was able to mold the Indian community in South Africa into a homogeneous group.

6 Gandhi returned to India in 1916 and began to work for Indian independence from Great Britain. Non-cooperation and peaceful resistance were Gandhi's weapons against the British troops. During this time there were several acts of violence and even massacres committed by the British troops. In retaliation to these acts, many Indians also committed acts of violence directed against the British troops.

7 Gandhi condemned acts of violence by both groups. He made many speeches where he advocated the principle that all violence was evil and could not be justified. While advocating non-violence, he also worked for complete individual, political, and spiritual independence for all Indians. All of his work came undone after a violent clash in the town of Chauri Chaura. Following this incident, Gandhi was tried for sedition and sent to prison for two years.

8 Gandhi remained out of the limelight until World War II broke out. During this time, he renewed his calls for Indian independence and called for Great Britain to "Quit India." Following World War II, India did gain independence from Great Britain. Gandhi had gained the respect and admiration of people from all over the world for his leadership in the non-violence movement. This movement and Gandhi's ideals of passive resistance would be modeled in other struggles throughout the world, including the civil rights movement in America.

---

fasting   the act of abstaining from food
London   the capital city of Great Britain

South Africa   a country at the southernmost tip of Africa

Vocabulary Study I

Match the word with its synonym.

1. unimpressive	a. advancement
2. tireless	b. visited often
3. promotion	c. determined
4. frequented	d. ordinary
5. brutal	e. cruel

Reading comprehension I

Main idea

What's the passage about?

a. The history of South Africa
b. The founding of India
c. Hindu practices
d. The life of Mahatma Gandhi

Detail questions

1. Gandhi was born _____.

   a. in England
   b. to a poor family
   c. into the royal family
   d. into a wealthy family

2. Gandhi went to South Africa to _____.

   a. work on a contract
   b. to study law
   c. work for civil rights
   d. to learn about other religions

3. Gandhi retuned to India and _____.

   a. started a trading company
   b. began to work for Indian independence
   c. began to work for South African independence
   d. began to work for British independence

Vocabulary Study II

Word root: crypt

1. **cryptology** = crypt (hidden) + logy (study)
   cryptic = crypt (hidden) + ic (having to do with)
   cryptogram = crypt (hidden) + gram (message)

2. **cryptology:** hidden, study → the coding or decodnig of secret messages
   crypic: hidden, having to do with → something with a puzzling or hidden meaning
   cryptogram: hidden, message → secret or coded message

3. Complete the following sentences choosing the right word.

cryptologist	cryptic	cryptogram

   a. A _____ is a person who works with codes.

   b. You need to know the code to understand a _____.

   c. I couldn't understand his _____ message.

Reading comprehension II

Inference and purpose

The purpose of this passage is to _____ .

   a. teach non-violence
   b. inform the reader about the history of India
   c. contrast the cultures of India, Great Britain, and South Africa
   d. inform the reader about the life and work of Mahatma Gandhi

Coherence

Look at the four squares [■] that indicate where the following sentence can be added to the passage below. Where would the sentence best fit?

This proved to be a difficult fight.

■ Gandhi had completed his year-long contract and was preparing to return to India. ■ He was attending a good-bye party held in his honor when he learned that legislation was being considered that would deny Indians the right to vote. He abandoned his plans to return to India; instead he stayed in South Africa and fought for Indian rights. ■ He was unsuccessful in stopping the voting ban law, but he was able to bring attention to the injustices that Indians faced in South Africa. ■

Listening comprehension

Main idea

What is the lecture mainly about?

    a. Gandhi's troubled marriage   b. Gandhi's exceptional talent

    c. The early life of Gandhi   d. Vegetarianism

Details

1. What is true about Kasturba?

    a. She taught English to Gandhi.

    b. She was just an ordinary student.

    c. She was Gandhi's wife.

    d. She was English.

2. What is true about Gandhi?

    a. He observed Hindu practices.

    b. He studied economics in London.

    c. He was in favor of injury to living things.

    d. He got married at age 30.

Paraphrasing

While in South Africa, he faced brutal discrimination that was commonly directed at Blacks and Indians.

Which of the sentences below best expresses the essential information in the highlighted sentence in the passage? Incorrect choices change the meaning in important ways or leave out essential information.

    a. Indians commonly discriminated against Blacks in South Africa.

    b. Whites commonly discriminated against Blacks and Indians in South Africa.

    c. Blacks commonly discriminated against Indians in South Africa.

    d. When in South Africa, Gandhi was treated in the same cruel way that Blacks and Indians frequently were.

Summary

Complete the following list by choosing the three true sentences about the passage.

-
-
-

a. Gandhi was raised in an orthodox Hindu family.

b. Gandhi thought South Africa was a model country because he saw no discrimination.

c. Gandhi worked for the unification of India with Great Britain.

d. Gandhi studied law in London.

e. Gandhi spent two years in prison.

f. While in London, Gandhi gave up his Hindu practices.

Speaking

Who do you most admire from history?

Model response

1. Fill in the blanks using the words in the box.

become	read	admire	poor	president	freed

   The person I _____ most is Abraham Lincoln. He was born
   _____ at a time when most people didn't learn to _____ and
   write. He worked hard and educated himself. He read every book he could find.
   He worked so hard that he grew up to _____ the President of the United
   States. When he was _____, he led the country through a civil war and
   _____ the slaves. I think he was a great man.

2. Using your own words, answer the question above. Then talk to the class.

Surfing

Pre-reading activity
1. Have you ever swum in the ocean?
2. Have you tried to ride a wave?
3. Have you seen people surfing?

1 Centuries before the first outsiders witnessed a person ride a plank of wood on a wave, the Hawaiians were **surfing**. Surfing was an important part of Hawaiian culture. The ruling class had **exclusive access** to the best beaches and the best boards. People who could ride a wave well were admired for their skill.

2 The first known non-Hawaiian to witness surfing was Jackson Crane, an American serving under the explorer Captain Cook. Captain Cook's crew saw the Hawaiians surfing during their visit in the late 1700s; on their return to Europe, stories of the wave riding Hawaiians spread. A few decades later in 1821, missionaries from **Scotland** and **Germany** arrived on the islands. The missionaries discouraged all Hawaiian traditions and cultural practices, including surfing. As a result, by the beginning of the twentieth century, surfing had almost disappeared. Only a few Hawaiians kept the art of riding waves and making boards **alive**.

3 In the early part of the twentieth century, surfing began to make a comeback. Many Hawaiians were angry over the overthrow of the Hawaiian Kingdom. As a way to show their anger, Hawaiians began to return to their traditional practices, including surfing. Surfing became popular in the islands again and began to spread to other shores.

---

surfing the sport of riding on a wave by standing on a surfboard
exclusive describing something that no others have a share

access the ability, right, or permission to enter, speak with, or use
Scotland a part of the United Kingdom located in the northern part of Great Britain above England

4 Duke Kahanamoku was well known for his five **Olympic** swimming medals: three gold medals and two silver medals. He became the person most responsible for spreading surfing throughout the world. Duke traveled to different parts of the world, particularly Australia and California, giving swimming and surfing demonstrations. While living in California, Duke saved eight sailors after their boat capsized. Using his surfboard, he was able to make quick trips to the shore and back. This not only further popularized the sport of surfing; it also established the tradition of lifeguards using surfboards.

5 Despite becoming widely known, there were still only a small number of surfers primarily in Hawaii, Australia, and California. In the 1960s, "beach movies" began the second wave of surfing growth. Surfing continued to grow slowly but was only practiced by a small group of avid devotees. One of the primary ways that surfing remained in the public eye was through "surf documentaries." These low budget films followed a group of actual surfer as they visited different beaches and rode waves. These films showed the skill of surfers and romanticized the surfers' lives.

6 The original Hawaiian surfboard was long and heavy, making quick moves on the waves difficult. In the early 1960s, the introduction of the short board revolutionized surfing. Now, surfers could make quick, almost acrobatic moves while riding the waves. "Hotdog" — showing off — surfing became popular and surf competitions began to appear at popular beach resorts. Sport surfing has evolved into a worldwide tour of events where top surfers are celebrities like soccer or basketball players. There is even talk of adding surfing to the Olympics.

Germany a country located in Central Europe west of France

alive in existence or operation

Olympic relating to the Olympic Games, a sports competition held every four years for amateur athletes from all over the world

Vocabulary Study I

Match the word with its synonym.

1. plank   a. board
2. exclusive   b. practice
3. discourage   c. restrain
4. overthrow   d. restricted
5. tradition   e. conquer

Reading comprehension I

Main idea

What's the passage about?

a. Surfing movies
b. The life of Duke Kahanamoku
c. The history of surfing
d. The history of the Hawaiian Islands

Detail questions

1. The first European to see surfing was _____.
   a. Jackson Crane   b. Captain Cook
   c. Duke Kahanamoku   d. a missionary from Scotland

2. Duke Kahanamoku was a champion _____.
   a. baseball player   b. surfer
   c. swimmer   d. soccer player

3. In the 1960s, the most popular places for surfing were _____.
   a. Hawaii, California, and England
   b. California, Australia, and England
   c. Jamaica, California, and Hawaii
   d. Hawaii, California, and Australia

Vocabulary Study II

Word root: dict

1. **predict** = pre (before) + dict (speak)

   contradict = contra (against) + dict (speak)

   edict = e (out) + dict (speak)

2. **predict:** before, speak → to something will happen before it happens

   contradict: against, speak → to speak the opposite of something

   edict: out, speak → a proclamation made by authority

3. Complete the following sentences choosing the right word.

predict	contradicted	edict

   a. The psychic is able to _____ the future.

   b. The King made an _____ that everyone must wear red on Tuesdays.

   c. The witness _____ her earlier testimony.

Reading comprehension II

Inference and purpose

It can be inferred from the passage that _____ .

   a. surfing is a dying sport

   b. surfing is a growing sport

   c. surfing will definitely be in the next Olympics

   d. surfing was invented in Australia

Coherence

Look at the four squares [■] that indicate where the following sentence can be added to the passage below. Where would the sentence best fit?

This would be the beginning of surfing's spread around the world.

■ In the early part of the twentieth century surfing began to make a comeback.
■ Many Hawaiians were angry over the overthrow of the Hawaiian Kingdom. ■ As a way to show their anger, Hawaiians began to return to their traditional practices, including surfing. Surfing became popular in the islands again and began to spread to other shores. ■ Duke Kahanamoku was well known for his five Olympic swimming medals: three gold medals and two silver medals.

Listening comprehension

Main idea

What is the lecture mainly about?

    a. Duke Kahanamoku's Olympic swimming medals

    b. Duke Kahanamoku's swimming skills

    c. Duke Kahanamoku's popularity

    d. Duke Kahanamoku's role in spreading surfing

Details

1. What is true about Duke Kahanamoku?

    a. He was poor at giving surfing demonstrations.

    b. While staying in California, he saved eighty people.

    c. He won fifteen Olympic swimming medals.

    d. He traveled to many parts of the world.

2. What is true about lifeguards?

    a. All of them are famous swimmers.
    b. Most of them work in California.

    c. They must entertain customers.
    d. They use surfboats.

Paraphrasing

Centuries before the first outsiders witnessed a person ride a plank of wood on a wave, the Hawaiians were surfing.

Which of the sentences below best expresses the essential information in the highlighted sentence in the passage? Incorrect choices change the meaning in important ways or leave out essential information.

    a. Hawaiians were surfing hundreds of years before the first Europeans saw it.

    b. Europeans brought surfing to the Hawaiians centuries before they learned to ride waves.

    c. Outsiders were the first to invent surfing centuries before the Hawaiians did.

    d. Hawaiians rode planks of wood for centuries before inventing surfing.

Summary

Complete the following list by choosing the three true sentences about the passage.

-
-
-

a. Surfing is the most popular sport in the world.

b. Today surfing is practiced in many parts of the world.

c. The first non-Hawaiian to witness surfing was Jackson Crane.

d. Surfing is an Olympic sport.

e. Duke Kahanamoku was an Olympic swimming champion.

f. Duke Kahanamoku invented surfing.

Speaking

What is your favorite sport?

Model response

1. Fill in the blanks using the words in the box.

> showed   places   favorite   friends   self-defense   healthy

My _____ sport is judo. Judo is very useful because it helps me stay _____ and it is a good form of _____. My father started to teach me judo when I was very young. I loved spending time with my father while he _____ me judo throws. Now, I go to a dojo three times a week for judo lessons. I have a lot of good _____ at my dojo; it is one of my favorite _____ to be.

2. Using your own words, answer the question above. Then talk to the class.

Audubon

Pre-reading activity
1. Do you know what a conservationist is?
2. Are there any endangered birds in your area?
3. Have you heard of the Audubon Society?

1 In the early 1900s, it was fashionable in America and Europe for women to wear hats decorated with feathers and sometimes even entire birds. This fashion created a market for the **plumes** of exotic birds. Plume hunters could make a great deal of money by hunting birds such as egrets and eagles. The slaughter of these and other types of birds brought some species to the verge of extinction.

2 If it weren't for the work of some far-sighted conservationists, many of the most beautiful birds of America would have been hunted to extinction. These early conservationists formed the Audubon Society to protect birds and their habitat in the wild. The founders of the Audubon Society drew their inspiration from the life and work of John James Audubon.

3 Audubon was born in 1785 in what is today **Haiti**. The son of a French captain and plantation owner, he was raised by his stepmother in Nantes, France. At an early age, he took an interest in birds, nature, and drawing. To escape conscription into **Napoleon**'s army, the 18-year-old Audubon was sent to live on his family's estate near Philadelphia. While living on his family's estate, he began to study and draw birds. It was during this period of his life that he conducted his first bird banding study. He tied strings around the legs of eastern phoebes and learned that the birds returned to the same nesting sites each year.

---

plume   feather
Haiti   a country of the West Indies that was once a French colony

Napoleon   18th century French general born in Corsica
rugged   full of hardship and trouble

4 After leaving his family estate, Audubon traveled to the frontier of Eastern Kentucky and set up a trade business. He ran a successful business for ten years until hard times forced him into bankruptcy. With limited prospects for his family, Audubon set off into the American wilderness with only a gun and his art materials. He spent most of the next five years traveling the western part of the United States, drawing and painting the birds that he found. This was a **rugged** life.

5 In 1826, Audubon took his collection of drawings and paintings to England. He was an **overnight** success. Europeans loved his depictions of the birds of America, but they loved his stories of life in the American wilderness even more. His drawings and paintings were printed in a book, which brought Audubon a modest amount of fame and wealth.

6 Audubon returned to America and made several more trips into the wilderness. His last book on the **mammals** of America was printed following his final trip west in 1843. Following his final trip, he settled in New York City with his wife and two sons. He died quietly at the age of 65 in 1851. Although Audubon died over a hundred and fifty years ago, his life and work still inspires young conservationists.

---

overnight occurring suddenly
mammal class of living things that have bodies covered with hair, feed the young with milk, and give birth to live young (with the exception of a few egg-laying animals)

Vocabulary Study I

Match the word with its synonym.

1. plume   a. chances
2. slaughter   b. killing
3. plantation   c. portrayal
4. prospects   d. feather
5. depiction   e. farm

Reading comprehension I

Main idea

What's the passage about?

a. The birds of America
b. Fashion trends in the early 1900s
c. The life of John James Audubon
d. Painting and drawing

Detail questions

1. The Audubon Society was formed to _____.
   a. protect hunter's rights   b. eradicate troublesome birds
   c. protect birds and their habitat d. eliminate hunting

2. Audubon went to America to _____.
   a. study birds   b. avoid going into the army
   c. to join the army   d. draw birds

3. Audubon went into the wilderness with _____.
   a. a group of servants   b. an army squad
   c. only art supplies   d. only a gun and art supplies

Word root: gress

1. **egress** = e (out of) + gress (to go, step)

   congress = con (together) + gress (to go, step)

   digress = di (away) + gress (to go, step)

2. **egress:** out of, to go → an exit

   congress: together, step → an assembly of representatives

   digress: away, to go → to go away from the topic

3. Complete the following sentences choosing the right word.

egress	congress	digress

   a. He will have to make an _____ to escape from prison.

   b. Every time we came close to solving the problem, he would _____ from the main topic.

   c. The elected representatives from all over the country will form the _____ .

Reading comprehension II

Inference and purpose

It can be inferred from the passage that _____ .

   a. the Audubon Society is over two hundred years old
   b. the Audubon Society has saved many birds
   c. the Audubon Society has millions of members
   d. the Audubon Society has caused the extinction of the predators of birds

Coherence

Look at the four squares [■] that indicate where the following sentence can be added to the passage below. Where would the sentence best fit?

He spent many hours out in the woods drawing what he saw.

Audubon was born in 1785 in what is today Haiti. ■ The son of a French captain and plantation owner, he was raised by his stepmother in Nantes, France. ■ At an early age, he took an interest in birds, nature and drawing. ■ To escape conscription into Napoleon's army the 18 year old Audubon was sent to live on his family's estate near Philadelphia. ■

Listening comprehension

Main idea

What is the lecture mainly about?

    a. Why Audubon was so famous in Haiti

    b. How Audubon left Philadelphia

    c. How Audubon began to study birds

    d. Why Audubon failed in his life

Details

1. What is true about Audubon's stepmother?

    a. She was French.
    b. She raised him.

    c. She was a natural scientist.
    d. She enjoyed growing flowers.

2. What is true about Audubon?

    a. He was a famous painter.

    b. He actively participated in war.

    c. As he grew older, he came to hate birds.

    d. He tied strings around the legs of some birds.

Paraphrasing

In 1826, Audubon took his collection of drawings and paintings to England.

Which of the sentences below best expresses the essential information in the highlighted sentence in the passage? Incorrect choices change the meaning in important ways or leave out essential information.

    a. In 1826, Audubon sent his collection of drawings and paintings to England.

    b. Audubon traveled with his collection of drawings and paintings to England in 1826.

    c. In 1826, Audubon went to England.

    d. In 1826, Audubon traveled with his drawings and paintings to Europe.

Summary

Complete the following list by choosing the three true sentences about the passage.

-
-
-

a. Audubon spent most of his childhood in France.

b. Audubon was born in America.

c. In his old age, Audubon returned to France.

d. Audubon published a book about mammals.

e. Audubon founded the Audubon Society.

f. Audubon made several trips into the wilderness.

Speaking

What is your favorite hobby?

Model response

1. Fill in the blanks using the words in the box.

> imagine   creative   because   different   playing   like

I have two favorite hobbies, _____ soccer and drawing. I love to play soccer _____ it is an exciting game, and when I play soccer I get to spend time with my friends. I like drawing just as much but for _____ reasons. I _____ to draw at times when I want to be alone. Drawing lets me be _____. I love to draw superheroes. I can _____ a superhero with special powers and then draw how he or she looks.

2. Using your own words, answer the question above. Then talk to the class.

The Gulf Stream

Pre-reading activity

1. Do you think turtles can migrate thousands of miles?
2. How far is it from the Caribbean Sea to Newfoundland?
3. Have you ever heard of the Indigo Highway?

1 Has anyone ever called you as slow as a turtle? If you are a slow runner, this is an **insult** you may have heard often. Most people think of turtles as among the slowest animals in the world. If this is true, how do loggerhead turtles make their journey from their home in the Caribbean Sea to their summer feeding grounds off the coast of Nova Scotia thousands of miles away each year?

2 The answer is that they catch a ride on a huge river of water: the Gulf Stream. The Gulf Stream is a current that originates south of the Florida peninsula and travels north along the east coast of the U.S.A. and ends off the Grand Banks of Newfoundland, where it joins the North Atlantic current. The loggerhead turtles, along with sharks, **tuna**, **swordfish**, and other marine life, catch a ride on this fast moving body of water. The Gulf Stream moves faster than the ocean water around it, so it moves large amounts of water like a river within the ocean. It is 50 to 100 miles wide (80.5 km to 161 km) and about a mile deep (1.6 km).

3 The Gulf Stream is so big that it moves more water than all of the world's rivers combined: 150 cubic meters of water per second. That's not just more water than all the rivers in the world; it's 100 times as much water as all the rivers of the world combined. Unlike rivers on land, you can't easily see the flow of water in the **Gulf** Stream, but if you know what to look for you can see its boundaries. The water in the Gulf Stream is bluer than the surrounding water. This blue color gives it the nickname the "Indigo Highway." The Gulf Stream or Indigo Highway also differs in temperature from the surrounding waters. It is warmer than the North Atlantic waters to the east and cooler than the Sargasso Sea to its west.

insult an impolite remark
tuna a type of fish that is eaten often and lives in temperate and tropical areas of the ocean

swordfish a large fish with an elongated upper jaw in the shape of a sword

4 The Gulf Stream not only plays an important role in the lives of marine life, it played a role in American history by affecting trade between the American colonies and Europe. In 1519, one of **Ponce de Leon**'s captains discovered that a ship could tremendously shorten the time it took to sail back to Europe by staying within the waters of the Gulf Stream. At the time this route was known as the "Highway of the Indies." Captains who knew of this time saver kept it a secret from their competitors.

5 A century after the discovery of the Gulf Stream, the Pilgrim's ship, the **Mayflower**, was also affected by the Gulf Stream. The Pilgrims sailed against the Gulf Stream forcing them to stay at sea for a lengthy 66 days and pushing the Mayflower north. This is why the Pilgrims landed at Plymouth Rock in what is today Massachusetts, instead of their original destination of Virginia.

6 One of the first people to study the Gulf Stream was Benjamin Franklin. While working in London just before the Revolutionary War, he heard complaints about the slowness of mail delivery from England. Franklin's cousin was the captain of a whaling ship from Nantucket, Massachusetts. By this time, all of the sea captains in North America knew about the Gulf Stream and used it to shorten their voyages. Some whaling captains had seen the British ships making slow progress sailing against the Gulf Stream and had tried to tell the British captains about the Indigo Highway, but the British thought the Americans were ignorant and rejected the advice. However, Franklin continued to study the Gulf Stream by measuring the temperature of the sea during his voyages across the Atlantic. With his cousin, he made remarkably accurate maps of the Gulf Stream.

7 The Gulf Stream is of great interest to oceanographers because of the great variety of life that uses its current. Today, the Gulf Stream is still used as a free ride by ocean travelers whether they are humans or animals.

....

gulf a portion of the sea that is partly enclosed by land

Ponce de Leon 15th century Spanish explorer who discovered the fountain of youth

Mayflower the ship in which the pilgrims sailed in the 17th century from England to Massachusetts

Vocabulary Study I

Match the word with its synonym.

1. combine
2. boundary
3. journey
4. voyage
5. ignorant

a. trip
b. join
c. border
d. unaware
e. cruise

Reading comprehension I

Main idea

What's the passage about?

a. Mail delivery to the American colonies
b. Benjamin Franklin
c. The Indigo Highway
d. Loggerhead turtles migration

Detail questions

1. Loggerhead turtles migrate from _____.
   a. Hawaii to Los Angeles
   b. the Caribbean Sea to the coast of Nova Scotia
   c. Nova Scotia to New York
   d. America to Mexico

2. The Gulf Stream moves more water than all of the _____.
   a. oceans in the world
   b. lakes in the world
   c. rivers in the world
   d. swimming pools in the world

3. Benjamin Franklin studied _____.
   a. whales
   b. mail delivery
   c. ships
   d. the Gulf Stream

Word root: dem, demo

1. **demophobia =** demo (people) + phobia (fear)
    democracy = demo (people) + cracy (rule)
    epidemic = epi (among) + dem (people) = ic (related to)

2. **demophobia:** people, fear → fear of crowds
    democracy: people, rule → rule by the people
    epidemic: among, people, related to → illness spread among people

3. Complete the following sentences choosing the right word.

demophobia	democracy	epidemic

    a. A person with _____ doesn't like crowds.
    b. The black plague was an _____ that killed thousands of people in Europe.
    c. In a _____ every person's vote is equal.

Reading comprehension II

Inference and purpose

It can be inferred from the passage that _____ .

   a. the Gulf Stream still affects ships
   b. Benjamin Franklin was a whale ship captain
   c. loggerhead turtles are the oldest animals on Earth
   d. there are Gulf Streams all over the world

Coherence

Look at the four squares [■] that indicate where the following sentence can be added to the passage below. Where would the sentence best fit?

The Gulf Stream isn't an actual river, but it moves water like one.

■ The answer is that they catch a ride on a huge river of water: the Gulf Stream. ■ The Gulf Stream is a current that originates south of the Florida peninsula and travels north along the east coast of the US and ends off the Grand Banks of Newfoundland where it joins the North Atlantic current. ■ The loggerhead turtles, along with sharks, tuna, swordfish, and other marine life, catch a ride on this fast moving body of water. ■

Listening comprehension

Main idea

What is the lecture mainly about?

- a. The environmental concerns affecting the Gulf Stream
- b. Ponce de Leon's captains
- c. The lives of marine life
- d. Benefits of using the Gulf Stream as a route

Details

1. What is true about the Gulf Stream?
   - a. It was the longest route in America.
   - b. Most ships avoided it because it was dangerous.
   - c. Everybody knew about its advantages.
   - d. It affected trade between some countries.

2. What is true about Highway of the Indies?
   - a. Ponce de Leon's captains let everybody know about the route.
   - b. It could shorten the time it took ships to sail back to Europe.
   - c. It did not affect the lives of marine life.
   - d. It was found in 1915.

Paraphrasing

> **The Gulf Stream not only plays an important role in the lives of marine life, it played a role in American history by affecting trade between the American colonies and Europe.**

Which of the sentences below best expresses the essential information in the highlighted sentence in the passage? Incorrect choices change the meaning in important ways or leave out essential information.

- a. American history was affected by the Gulf Stream and marine life.
- b. The Gulf Stream plays an important role in American history and played a role in the lives of marine animals.
- c. The Gulf Stream only affects marine life, but American history was affected by trade with Europe.
- d. The Gulf Stream is important to marine life, and it played a role in American history by impacting trade with Europe.

Summary

Complete the following list by choosing the three true sentences about the passage.

> -
> -
> -

a. The Gulf Stream runs from the tip of South America to the Arctic Ocean.

b. Other names for the Gulf Stream are the Indigo Highway and the Indies Highway.

c. Benjamin Franklin's father was a whale ship captain.

d. Loggerhead turtles migrate from the Caribbean Sea to the coast of Nova Scotia.

e. The Mayflower was Benjamin Franklin's cousin's ship.

f. The Mayflower landed at Plymouth Rock.

Speaking

If you could go anywhere in the world, where would you go?

Model response

1. Fill in the blanks using the words in the box.

> anywhere　　wonderful　　team　　cheer　　love　　person

If I could go _____, I would go to England. I would go to England because I _____ soccer, and Manchester United is my favorite _____. I would go to see all of the games that I could. While I was there I would _____ for the team and try to meet the players. It would be _____ to see all of my favorite players in _____.

2. Using your own words, answer the question above. Then talk to the class.

The American Pastime

Pre-reading activity

1. What sports are popular in your country?
2. Have you ever played baseball?
3. Do you know who invented baseball?

1 Baseball has long been known as the American pastime. Every **schoolyard** throughout the country has at least one baseball diamond, and on any summer's day you can watch baseball games being played. Every American city and town has baseball leagues for children to adults, so everyone can enjoy the national game. Baseball has been played in America for over a hundred and fifty years. Today, its popularity is not limited to the U.S.A.; there are professional baseball leagues in many other countries including Japan, Korea, and throughout **Latin America**. Baseball is one of the most popular American exports to the rest of the world, but is baseball really an American invention?

2 Ask most Americans who invented baseball and they will answer "Abner Doubleday." The legend says that Abner Doubleday invented baseball in the small town of Cooperstown, New York, in 1839. This was such a widely held belief that the baseball hall of fame was built at the supposed site of the invention of the game in Cooperstown. Modern historians can find no evidence that Doubleday invented baseball. Doubleday was a war hero who wrote **extensively**, but in all of his writings there is no mention of baseball. Also, Doubleday never lived in Cooperstown and may have never even visited the town. It is now believed that the legend of Doubleday's invention of baseball was created to settle an argument over who invented the national game.

---

schoolyard a playground or sports field near a school

Latin America parts of the American continents south of the United States where Spanish, Portuguese, and French are spoken

3 The story of how Doubleday invented baseball became popular in 1908; fifteen years after his death, after a panel of baseball executives wrote a report endorsing the story. The only evidence in support of the Doubleday legend was the **testimony** of Abner Green, who was a five year old resident of Cooperstown in 1839. Abner Green's story is questionable because he later murdered his wife and died in a prison for the criminally **insane**. After historians **discredited** Doubleday as the inventor of baseball, their next job was to answer the question of who invented baseball.

4 The invention of baseball has been open to much debate, but most historians agree that baseball wasn't invented but evolved from several earlier games. Games played with a bat and ball were popular in Great Britain for centuries prior to the first recorded baseball game. Some of these games were called *stool ball*, *poison ball*, and *goal ball*. These games were widely played in Great Britain and early America. These games were similar but the rules of these games varied from town to town. Historians now believe that as Americans became more mobile, moving easily from town to town, they began to agree on the rules for a game that would later become baseball.

5 The first published rules of baseball were written by Alexander Joy Cartwright in 1845. These rules were written for a New York City baseball club called the Knickerbockers. The so-called Knickerbocker rules evolved into the rules of modern baseball. On June 3, 1953, the United States Congress officially credited Cartwright with the invention of baseball. Although some people still argue that Cartwright didn't invent baseball but simply wrote down the rules, he was inducted into the baseball hall of fame at the site of the Doubleday legend, Cooperstown, New York.

---

extensively in a great amount, number, or degree

insane not sound in mind, mentally ill, crazy

discredit reject as false, cause to be disbelieved

testimony statement or declaration of a witness

Vocabulary Study I

Match the word with its synonym.

1. pastime
2. modern
3. testimony
4. executive
5. mobile

a. movable
b. spoken proof
c. entertainment
d. contemporary
e. boss

Reading comprehension I

Main idea

What's the passage about?

a. The life of Alexander Cartwright
b. Games played with a bat and ball
c. The life of Abner Doubleday
d. The invention of baseball

Detail questions

1. _____ has been called America's national pastime.

a. Soccer
c. Baseball

b. Basketball
d. Football

2. The U.S. congress declared _____ the inventor of baseball.

a. Abner Doubleday
c. Alexander Cartwright

b. Abner Green
d. Abraham Lincoln

3. The first written rules of baseball were published in _____.

a. 1855
c. 1835

b. 1845
d. 1865

Vocabulary Study II

Word root: ped, pede, pedo

1. **impede =** im (not) + pede (foot)
    expedite = ex (away from) + ped (foot) + ite (connected with)
    pedometer = pedo (foot) + meter (measure)

2. **impede:** not, foot → prevent movement
    expedite: away from, foot, connected with → to speed up
    pedometer: foot, measure → an instrument that measure distances walked

3. Complete the following sentences choosing the right word.

impeded	expedited	pedometer

    a. The storm _____ the ship's progress.

    b. When I walk, I use a _____ to measure how far I have gone.

    c. The judge insisted that the order be _____ immediately.

Reading comprehension II

Inference and purpose

It can be inferred from the passage that _____ .

    a. baseball is not popular in Europe

    b. baseball is popular in Europe

    c. baseball is not popular in Japan

    d. baseball is the most popular sport in the world

Coherence

Look at the four squares [■] that indicate where the following sentence can be added to the passage below. Where would the sentence best fit?

Although this is a widely held belief, it has been shown to be incorrect.

■ Ask most Americans who invented baseball and they will answer, "Abner Doubleday." ■ The legend says that Abner Doubleday invented baseball in the small town of Cooperstown New York in 1839. ■ This was such a widely held belief that the baseball hall of fame was built at the supposed site of the invention of the game in Cooperstown. Modern historians can find no evidence that Doubleday invented baseball. Doubleday was a war hero who wrote extensively, but in all of his writings there is no mention of baseball. ■

Listening comprehension

Main idea

What is the lecture mainly about?

    a. The question of who shot Abner Green

    b. Cooperstown in 1839

    c. The importance of history in everyday life

    d. The question of who really invented baseball

Details

1. What is true about Doubleday?

    a. He murdered his wife.

    b. He was an expert in baseball.

    c. Many people believed that he invented baseball.

    d. He was found insane.

2. What is true about Abner Green?

    a. People believed that he invented baseball.

    b. He committed a crime.

    c. All the people believed his testimony.

    d. He once lived in Australia.

Paraphrasing

Every American city and town has baseball leagues for children to adults so everyone can enjoy the national game.

Which of the sentences below best expresses the essential information in the highlighted sentence in the passage? Incorrect choices change the meaning in important ways or leave out essential information.

    a. Every American city has a professional baseball team so everyone can enjoy the national game.

    b. There are baseball leagues for children and adults in every town, so every American plays baseball.

    c. Every American can enjoy baseball because there are leagues for children and adults in every city and town.

    d. Every American plays baseball because there are baseball teams in every city and town.

Summary

Complete the following list by choosing the three true sentences about the passage.

-
-
-

a. Many people believe that Abner Doubleday invented baseball.

b. Abner Doubleday wrote about inventing baseball.

c. Baseball was first played in 1908.

d. Alexander Cartwright wrote the first published rule of baseball.

e. There are professional baseball leagues in Great Britain.

f. Baseball is popular in Japan.

Speaking

What things do you enjoy that came from other countries?

Model response

1. Fill in the blanks using the words in the box.

> many   country   getting   activity   become   animation

I live in America; there are _____ things in America that came from other parts of the world. My favorite foods come from China and India, and I love Japanese _____. But my favorite _____ that came from another _____ is tae kwon do. Tae kwon do is a martial art that comes from Korea. I've been studying it for three years, and I'm _____ better all the time. Someday, I hope to pass my black belt test and _____ a tae kwon do instructor.

2. Using your own words, answer the question above. Then talk to the class.

The California Gold Rush

1 Johann Sutter was a **Swiss** immigrant who arrived in **California** in 1839. He settled in what is today Sacramento and built a thriving business based on farming and trade. Always looking to expand his business interests, he hired James Marshall in 1848, to build a mill along the banks of the American River. This decision would change Johann Sutter's life and the history of California.

2 On January 4, 1848, while working on Sutter's Mill, James Marshall picked up a piece of shiny metal out of the American River. He took the metal to Sutter to have it analyzed; Marshall's suspicion was confirmed. James Marshall had found gold. Sutter was a shrewd businessman; he knew that once word spread that gold had been discovered, there would be a rush to mine for gold. Sutter feared that his workers would leave their jobs and that his fields would be overrun by gold prospectors, so he and Marshall agreed to keep the discovery a secret.

3 The men were able to keep their secret for a short time, but in the fall of 1848 Marshall paid for a drink with gold dust. People began to ask questions and the word of the gold discovery quickly spread. By the end of 1848, news of gold in California had spread across the country. The California gold rush was on.

4 In 1849, 300,000 people from all over the country and world came to California in search of gold; these gold prospectors became known as 49ers. They came to California by sailing ship or overland by covered wagon, often facing severe hardships along the way. In California, they found the streams and rivers teeming with prospectors, and once small towns had turned into boomtowns.

Swiss relating to an inhabitant of Switzerland, a country in Europe located between Germany and France

California a state located on the far west coast of the United States

5 There wasn't enough housing to deal with the sudden influx of so many people. The miners had to live in tents or wood shanties. People had "gold fever" so bad that ships that sailed into **San Francisco Bay** were often abandoned by their crews and left anchored in the bay. At the height of the gold rush, it was said that a person could walk across the bay on all of the abandoned ships.

6 Many fortunes were made from the gold rush, but only a few from gold. Most of the 49ers returned home or found other work, never finding more than small amounts of gold. The fortunes were made by farsighted people who set up stores to supply the 300,000 newly arrived miners. One of these people was Samuel Brannan, a San Francisco newspaper reporter. He got early word of the gold find before it was published in the newspapers. He immediately opened a store to sell prospecting equipment. Once his store was open, he walked down the streets of San Francisco holding a vial of gold yelling "Gold, Gold, Gold, from the American River."

7 By the mid 1850s, gold was becoming hard to find. People who had come to get rich on gold turned to other types of work. "Gold fever" was over, but California had just begun to grow. Towns were founded where none had been before. **Prior** to the gold rush, few people had heard of California, but by 1850 it had been admitted to the United States as the 31st state. Discovery of silver in neighboring **Nevada** in 1859 signaled the end of the California gold rush. Those who were still prospecting for gold left for Nevada, but the majority stayed in California and built the state.

8 Ironically, the two men who started the gold rush, James Marshall and Johann Sutter, never made a living from gold. Sutter was right in his fears of the gold rush. His workers did leave their jobs and his fields were overrun, destroying his once prosperous business empire. Marshall was forced from his land by the onslaught of prospectors and never profited from his discovery.

....

San Francisco Bay   a bay in San Francisco, a city in California, that connects to the Pacific Ocean

prior   before
Nevada   a state in the western United States east of California

Vocabulary Study I

Match the word with its synonym.

1. thrive
2. shrewd
3. abandon
4. influx
5. fortune

a. incursion
b. wealth
c. forsake
d. bloom
e. smart

Reading comprehension I

Main idea

What's the passage about?

a. Johann Sutter's business
b. The California gold rush
c. California
d. James Marshall

Detail questions

1. James Marshall discovered gold in _____.

a. San Francisco
b. Sacramento
c. the American River
d. the Mississippi River

2. Prospectors who came to California in search of gold were called _____.

a. gold seekers
b. 59ers
c. 49ers
d. 39ers

3. Silver was discovered in Nevada in _____.

a. 1859
b. 1850
c. the mid 1850s
d. 1950

Vocabulary Study II

Word root: eco

1. **ecology** = eco (house) + logy (study)
   ecohazard = eco (house) + hazard (chance)
   economy = eco (house) + nom (management) + y (act of)

2. **ecology:** house, study → study of the environment
   ecohazard: house, chance → threat to habitat
   economy: house, management, act of → management of resources

3. Complete the following sentences choosing the right word.

ecology	ecohazard	economy

   a. The _____ of the Earth is in danger from global warming.

   b. An oil spill is an _____.

   c. When the stock market goes up, the _____ is doing well.

Reading comprehension II

Inference and purpose

It can be inferred from the passage that _____ .

   a. James Marshall became rich after finding gold
   b. San Francisco Bay still has many abandoned ships in it
   c. the gold rush helped California become a state
   d. the gold rush is still going on

Coherence

Look at the four squares [■] that indicate where the following sentence can be added to the passage below. Where would the sentence best fit?

Prospecting for gold was hard work that usually resulted in failure.

■ Many fortunes were made from the gold rush, but only a few from gold. ■ Most of the 49ers returned home or found other work never finding more than small amounts of gold. The fortunes were made by farsighted people who setup stores to supply the 300,000 newly arrived miners. ■ One of these people was Samuel Brannan a San Francisco newspaper reporter. He got early word of the gold find before it was published in the newspapers. ■

56

Listening comprehension

Main idea

What is the lecture mainly about?

    a. Those who invented blue jeans during the gold rush

    b. Those who improved technology during the gold rush

    c. Those who made a fortune during the gold rush

    d. Those who lost their money during the gold rush

Details

1. What is true about fortyniners?

    a. Most of them found large amounts of gold.

    b. Most of them had worked as newspaper reporters.

    c. Most of them opened large stores.

    d. Most of them couldn't get rich.

2. What is true about Samuel Brannan?

    a. He was a TV reporter.

    b. He tried to find gold.

    c. He sold blue jeans and wagon covers.

    d. He made a lot of money

Paraphrasing

They came to California by sailing ship or overland by covered wagon, often facing severe hardships along the way.

Which of the sentences below best expresses the essential information in the highlighted sentence in the passage? Incorrect choices change the meaning in important ways or leave out essential information.

    a. Sailing ship and covered wagon were the most common ways for them to get to California.

    b. The journey to California was the hardest thing they had done, whether they came by sailing ship or by covered wagon.

    c. They faced the most hardship by coming overland in covered wagons.

    d. They dealt with many difficulties whether they came by sailing ship or overland in covered wagons.

Summary

Complete the following list by choosing the three true sentences about the passage.

-
-
-

a. 300,000 people came to California seeking gold.

b. Gold was discovered in California in 1948.

c. Many people became rich from gold.

d. Many ships were abandoned in San Francisco Bay.

e. Everyone who came looking for gold left within a year.

f. Gold was discovered in the American River.

Speaking

Have you ever had to look very hard for something?

Model response

1. Fill in the blanks using the words in the box.

| parents | imagination | department | ran | big | find |

Once when I was little, I got lost in a big _____ store. As soon as I realized that my _____ weren't near me, I got really scared. I looked everywhere for them, but I couldn't _____ them. Because I was so little, my _____ started to go wild. I thought I would never see them again and I would live in the store. Just as I gave up hope and started to cry, I saw my dad. I _____ as fast as I could and we gave each other a _____ hug. It sure felt good.

2. Using your own words, answer the question above. Then talk to the class.

Auroras

Pre-reading activity
1. What do you see when you look in the night sky?
2. Have you ever seen a strange light in the sky?
3. Have you heard of an aurora?

1 Auroras are spectacular multi-colored lights that can be seen in the night sky near the South and North Poles. These beautiful lights appear as pink, red, yellow, and green bands of light that seem to shoot up into the night sky. They were named after the **Roman** goddess of the dawn, Aurora. Lights in the Northern sky are called aurora borealis, from the **Greek** name for the north wind, Boreas. Auroras in the Southern sky are called aurora australis, from the **Latin** word for south, australis.

2 There are many legends that attempt to explain the auroras. Thomas Bulfinch said that **Norse** mythology attributed the Northern lights to warriors riding horses in the night sky. Their shields and spears produced the light shows. The Scandinavian word to describe the auroras translates as "herring flash." They believed that the night lights were reflected off huge schools of herring.

3 The Sami people of Scandinavia thought the auroras were something to be feared. They believed that if a person laughed at the lights, the light would descend upon that person and kill them. Ancient people made many creative stories to explain the auroras. Modern science was only recently able to adequately explain the causes of the polar light shows.

4 Auroras are created when either negatively or positively charged particles, called ions, collide with atoms in the Earth's upper atmosphere, above 80 kilometers. Clouds of ions are called plasma; clouds of plasma travel from the sun at speeds of 300 to 1200 kilometers per second. The movement of charged

---

Roman relating to the ancient Roman Empire, whose capital was the city of Rome in modern day Italy

Greek pertaining to the country of Greece located in Southeastern Europe on the Balkan peninsula

particles from the Sun is called the solar wind. The solar wind moves out from the Sun in all directions, but when the plasma moves close to the Earth's magnetic field, it lines up with the magnetic field lines. This is what gives the auroras their curtain-like appearance. When the ions in the solar wind hit atoms in the Earth's upper atmosphere, they become excited and release their energy. This energy is released as light, ultraviolet, infrared, and X-rays; we see the light rays as auroras.

5 Auroras are beautiful to look at, but they can cause some problems with navigation, communication, and electronic devices. Auroras release a huge amount of **electromagnetic** energy. One Aurora display can release as much energy as the entire U.S. uses in a day. The energy released in an aurora can travel along with the Earth's magnetic field for thousands of miles. This electromagnetic energy can disrupt radio communications, cause compasses to point in the wrong direction, cause power systems to fail, and cause computers to malfunction. On one occasion, taxi drivers in **Alaska** received radio transmissions from a cab company in New Jersey, over five thousand miles away.

6 Perhaps the greatest light show in history occurred for a few nights in the late summer of 1859. During these nights, the aurora was so brilliant that people reported that they could read newspapers in the middle of the night by the aurora's light. The aurora could be seen throughout North America, much of Asia, Australia, and parts of South America. The aurora released so much electromagnetic energy that telegraph lines were disrupted, but some lines which ran along the magnetic fields were able to remain in use. In fact, these telegraph lines were able to draw electricity from the aurora and run without their batteries. People relied much less on electronic devices in the 1800s than we do today. Imagine how disruptive an aurora of that size would be today.

Latin the language spoken in Ancient Rome
Norse relating to ancient Scandinavia
electromagnetic relating to the magnetism that is produced by electric charge in motion

Alaska a state located in northwestern North America west of Canada

Vocabulary Study I

Match the word with its synonym.

1. spectacular   a. quantity
2. mythology   b. unbind
3. plasma   c. legend
4. amount   d. amazing
5. release   e. mass

Reading comprehension I

Main idea

What's the passage about?

a. The Earth's magnetic field   b. Auroras
c. Solar wind   d. Norse mythology

Detail questions

1. Auroras are caused by _____.
   a. schools of herring
   b. warrior's shields and spears
   c. charged ions from the Sun hitting atoms
   d. the polar ice caps

2. Clouds of ions are called _____.
   a. storms   b. thunderclouds
   c. plasma   d. auroras

3. The biggest aurora known happened in _____.
   a. 1962   b. 1862
   c. 1959   d. 1859

Vocabulary Study II

Word root: form

1. **conform =** con (together) + form (shape)
   reform = re (again) + form (shape)
   nonconformist = non (not) + con (together) + form (shape) ist (person)

2. **conform:** together, shape → to act together
   reform: again, shape → to remake, to make better
   nonconformist: not, together, shape, person → a person who acts individually

3. Complete the following sentences choosing the right word.

conform	reformed	nonconformist

   a. The healthcare system must be _____ to serve the people better.

   b. His original ideas made him a _____ .

   c. To _____ with the other students, he had to wear the same clothes.

Reading comprehension II

Inference and purpose

The purpose of the passage is to inform the reader about _____ .

   a. solar winds
   b. the Earth's magnetic field
   c. auroras
   d. Norse mythology

Coherence

Look at the four squares [■] that indicate where the following sentence can be added to the passage below. Where would the sentence best fit?

This can be dangerous in today's society where we depend so much on technology.

■ Auroras are beautiful to look at, but they can cause some problems with navigation, communication, and electronic devices. ■ Auroras release a huge amount of electromagnetic energy. ■ One Aurora display can release as much energy as the entire USA uses in a day. The energy released in an aurora can travel along with the Earth's magnetic field for thousands of miles. This electromagnetic energy can disrupt radio communications, cause compasses to point in the wrong direction, cause power systems to fail, and cause computer to malfunction. On one occasion taxi drivers in Alaska received radio transmissions from a Cab company in New Jersey over five thousand miles away. ■

Listening comprehension

Main idea

What is the lecture mainly about?

- a. The importance of the sun in our lives
- b. The Earth's magnetic field
- c. How auroras occur
- d. The solar wind

Details

1. What is true about ions?

   - a. They cannot cause auroras to occur.
   - b. They never collide with atoms in the earth's atmosphere.
   - c. They do not contain any energy.
   - d. They are electrically charged particles.

2. What is true about auroras?

   - a. Whenever it rains, they occur.
   - b. They usually look like curtains.
   - c. They occur only in winter.
   - d. They are dark rays.

Paraphrasing

Auroras are created when either negatively or positively charged particles, called ions, collide with atoms in the Earth's upper atmosphere, above 80 km.

Which of the sentences below best expresses the essential information in the highlighted sentence in the passage? Incorrect choices change the meaning in important ways or leave out essential information.

- a. In the Earth's upper atmosphere, negatively and positively charged particles called ions hit atoms, causing auroras.
- b. Auroras are made when ions hit the earth.
- c. Auroras are created when positively charged particles called ions hit the Earth's atmosphere.
- d. The explosions that happen when ions hit the earth create auroras.

Summary

Complete the following list by choosing the three true sentences about the passage.

-
-
-

a. Auroras near the South Pole are called auroras australis.

b. The solar wind blows from north to south

c. The aurora in 1859 was so bright that people could read a newspaper at night.

d. Scientists still don't know what causes auroras.

e. The Sami people thought that auroras were something to be feared.

f. Auroras are most common around the equator.

Speaking

What is the most beautiful thing you have ever seen?

Model response

1. Fill in the blanks using the words in the box.

> wear   before   beautiful   antique   gave   meaning

The most _____ thing I've ever seen is a ring that my Grandmother _____ me. It has an opal set in gold. It was given to my Grandmother by her mother. I don't know how old the ring is but it must be very old, at least one-hundred years old. I guess that makes it an _____. Although the ring looks beautiful, the real beauty of it for me is the _____ it has. My Grandmother gave it to me _____ she died, so whenever I _____ the ring I think of my Grandmother. This makes it a very beautiful ring to me.

2. Using your own words, answer the question above. Then talk to the class.

The Running of the Bulls

Pre-reading activity
1. Have you ever seen a bull?
2. Have you heard of people running with bulls?
3. Would you run in front of a charging bull?

1 Imagine running in front of a two-ton animal that is equipped with a pair of sharp horns. People from all over the world come to Pamplona, **Spain**, every year to do exactly that. In Spanish it's the annual *el encierro*, or running of the bulls festival. The el encierro is a nine-day festival where the bulls are run through a section of town into the city's bullring. Unlike **bullfighting**, where only professionals can **partake**, anyone is allowed to run with the bulls during the festival.

2 The origin of this custom is the transport of the bulls from corrals to the bullring in town for the bullfights. While the bulls were being herded through town, youngsters would jump in among the bulls to show off. Injuries during the running of the bulls are common both to people being run over or gored by the bulls and to the bulls that often slip on the cobblestone streets. Since 1924, there have been 15 deaths; the most recent death occurred in 1995, when an American tourist was gored.

3 In preparation for the running of the bulls, the town's people place wooden and iron barricades along the route that the bulls are to run. These barriers have gaps in them wide enough for a person to jump through but too narrow for a bull. This allows the runners an **avenue** of escape if the bulls get too close and prevents the bulls from running all over the town.

Spain a country located in western Europe
bullfighting a Spanish, Portuguese or Latin American spectacle in which a matador fights a bull and eventually kills it

partake to take part in, participate
avenue a means of access or attainment
steer a male ox castrated before sexual maturity and raised for beef

4 At the start of the running, a rocket is set off to alert the runners that the bulls have been released. As the running herd of bulls approach, shouts of "Ahi va! Ahi va!" ("There it goes, there it goes") can be heard, as a warning that the bulls are near. Some people head for the barricades as the bulls come; others stay in the narrow cobblestone streets and prepare to run to stay ahead of the bulls.

5 As the bulls approach, the people begin to run. For a short time, they stay ahead of the bulls, but the bulls soon overtake them. At this point people and bulls are running together. A good run is when the bulls run swiftly through the streets, but often a bull will become distracted or separated from the herd. Many people think it is good luck to touch a bull during the running, but experienced runners disapprove of this practice because it distracts the bulls from the running. It is when bulls become distracted and are separated from the herd that they are the most dangerous. A lone bull will become frightened and may try to gore anyone who comes near. To collect the bulls that have become separated from the main herd, **steers** are released to run the same route as the bulls. The stray bulls will join the steers and finish the run

6 The running of the bulls ends when the bulls and some of the runners arrive in the bullring. The bulls are guided out into a nearby corral. Some bulls and **calves** are released back into the bullring where some runners will entertain the crowd by taunting them. What started as a local event has turned into a cultural phenomenon with worldwide appeal. The running of the bulls has captured the imagination of would-be adventurers from all over the world, and has been immortalized in Ernest Hemmingway's works "The Sun Also Rises" and "Death in the Afternoon."

calf   the young of the domestic cow

Vocabulary Study I

Match the word with its synonym.

1. exactly
2. festival
3. gore
4. narrow
5. immortal

a. celebration
b. constricted
c. living forever
d. precisely
e. pierce

Reading comprehension I

Main idea

What's the passage about?

a. Bulls
b. Ernest Hemmingway
c. A festival held in Pamplona, Spain
d. Bullfighting

Detail questions

1. A _____ announces the beginning of the running of the bulls.

   a. rocket
   b. whistle
   c. shout
   d. gun shot

2. The running of the bulls takes place every _____.

   a. month
   b. four years
   c. year
   d. ten years

3. The running of the bulls ends when the bulls _____.

   a. run into the sea
   b. run into a corral
   c. have outrun all of the people
   d. arrive in the bullring

Vocabulary Study II

Word root: cide

1. **herbicide =** herb (plant) + cide (kill)
   suicide = sui (self) + cide (kill)
   genocide = geno (race, kind) + cide (kill)

2. **herbicide:** plant, kill → substance used for killing plants
   suicide: self, kill → deliberately killing oneself
   genocide: race, kill → killing a large group of people

3. Complete the following sentences choosing the right word.

herbicide	suicide	genocide

   a. Someone who is very depressed might try to commit _____ .

   b. The Nazis committed _____ against the Jews.

   c. The farmer used a _____ to kill unwanted plants.

Reading comprehension II

Inference and purpose

The purpose of the passage is to inform the reader about _____ .

   a. sports in Spain   b. festivals in Spain

   c. the running of the bulls   d. bulls

Coherence

Look at the four squares [■] that indicate where the following sentence can be added to the passage below. Where would the sentence best fit?

The bulls begin their run down the narrow streets of Pamplona.

■ At the start of the running, a rocket is set off to alert the runners that the bulls have been released. ■ As the running herd of bulls approach, shouts of "Ahi va! Ahi va!" ("There it goes, there it goes") can be heard, as a warning that the bulls are near. ■ Some people head for the barricades as the bulls come; others stay in the narrow cobblestone streets and prepare to run to stay ahead of the bulls. ■

Listening comprehension

Main idea

What is the lecture mainly about?
  a. Why bulls are violent
  b. How to reduce instances of injuries
  c. The origin of a special festival
  d. The history of bullfights

Details

1. What is true about the festival?
  a. It is a festival worshiping cows.
  b. It is related to the transporting of the bulls.
  c. It is a festival celebrating American history.
  d. It is a festival only for proud children.

2. What is true about 1995?
  a. In that year, the festival ended.
  b. In that year, the festival attracted thousands of people.
  c. In that year, the festival claimed 15 lives.
  d. In that year, an American tourist was killed by a bull.

Paraphrasing

At the start of the running, a rocket is set off to alert the runners that the bulls have been released.

Which of the sentences below best expresses the essential information in the highlighted sentence in the passage? Incorrect choices change the meaning in important ways or leave out essential information.

  a. At the start of the running, the bulls set off a rocket, and then they are released.
  b. A rocket is set off to get the bulls running.
  c. As the bulls are released to start the running, a rocket is set off to warn the runners that the bulls are coming.
  d. The runners set off a rocket to warn the bulls that the running has begun.

Summary

Complete the following list by choosing the three true sentences about the passage.

-
-
-

a. The running of the bulls occurs in Pamplona, Spain

b. People who touch the bulls during the running help the bulls find the bullring.

c. Fifteen people have died running with the bulls since 1924.

d. A rocket is set off at the beginning of the running of the bulls.

e. The tradition of running with the bulls began as a religious ceremony.

f. The running of the bulls takes place in Mexico.

Speaking

Have you ever seen anyone do anything dangerous?

Model response

1. Fill in the blanks using the words in the box.

> together   escape   dangerous   amazing   pool   impossible

I once saw a man on TV do something that looked very _____. He had his assistants handcuff his hands and feet _____; then they locked him in a big glass box. The man was going to try to _____ from the box. I thought it looked _____. Then they lowered the glass box with the man inside into a _____ of water. If the man didn't escape in time, he could drown. This looked very dangerous to me. The man escaped in less than a minute. I thought it was _____ but too dangerous for me. I would never do anything like that.

2. Using your own words, answer the question above. Then talk to the class.

12

Mount Everest

Pre-reading activity
1. Have you ever thought of going on an adventure?
2. Would you want to climb a mountain?
3. What is the highest mountain in the world?

1 What could bring a man born into a poor family from **Nepal** and a man from **New Zealand** together and make them part of history? Tenzing Norgay was a Nepalese **Sherpa** when he met Sir Edmund Hillary, a New Zealand explorer. Although they came from very different backgrounds, both men shared a passion for the adventure of mountain climbing. They met near the foot of the highest mountain in the world — Mt. Everest — with one goal in mind: to be the first people to step foot on the top of the world.

2 Mount Everest is located on the border of Nepal and **Tibet**, China. It is 29,029 feet (8,848 meters) high — the highest point on Earth. Thus far, 2,062 people have successfully climbed the mountain and 203 have died on the mountain. The conditions on the mountain are so severe that most of the people who have died on the mountain have been left where they died because it is too dangerous to try to carry the body down the mountain. Although people climb Mount Everest every year, in 1953 no one had successfully scaled the mountain. In 1924, George Mallory and Andrew Irvine made one of the first serious attempts to reach the summit of Everest; neither man returned. In the following years, there were many attempts to conquer Everest, but none were successful until Hillary and Norgay met.

Nepal a country in the Himalayas between India and Southwest China

New Zealand a country located in the South Pacific southeast of Australia

3 In 1953, John Hunt returned to Everest for the seventh time to lead the ninth British expedition on the mountain. The team climbed to a base camp near the summit. As the team leader, John Hunt chose two teams of two to attempt the final **assault** on the summit. The first team, Tom Bordello and Charles Evans, climbed to within 300 feet of their goal, before having to turn back due to exhaustion. Three days later, the second team made their attempt on the mountain. At 11:30 on May 29, 1953, Edmund Hillary and Tenzing Norgay stepped foot on the top of the world. Once on the summit, they stayed there for only fifteen minutes. Norgay buried some sweets in the snow, and Hillary left a cross. Hillary took some pictures of Norgay. There are no pictures of Hillary at the summit because Hillary didn't think Norgay knew how to **operate** the camera. The news of their accomplishment quickly reached around the world and made the two men instant celebrities.

4 Following the first successful ascent of Everest, Hillary continued mountain climbing and exploring. He climbed ten other peaks in the Himalayas. In 1958, he was part of an expedition to the South Pole, and in 1985 he accompanied Neil Armstrong, the first man to step on the moon, in a flight over the Arctic Ocean to the North Pole, becoming the first man to stand on both poles and the top of the world. Tenzing Norgay became the director of the Himalayan Mountaineering Institute and continued to climb in the Himalayas. The two men from different backgrounds who met and made history remained good friends until Tenzing's death in 1986.

Sherpa a member of the Himalayan people that live in Tibet and Nepal that are famous for their mountain climbing skills

Tibet an autonomous region of southwest China

assault a sudden attack

operate to work or use a machine, apparatus, etc.

Vocabulary Study I

Match the word with its synonym.

1. explorer
2. passion
3. summit
4. severe
5. operate

a. desire
b. harsh
c. someone who investigates the unknown
d. maneuver
e. the highest point

Reading comprehension I

Main idea

What's the passage about?

a. Edmund Hillary
b. Tenzing Norgay
c. The men who first climbed Mount Everest
d. Mount Everest

Detail questions

1. Tenzing Norgay is from _____.
   a. New Zealand
   b. China
   c. Australia
   d. Nepal

2. Mount Everest was first climbed in _____.
   a. 1867
   b. 1953
   c. 1899
   d. 1963

3. Norgay and Hillary left _____ on the top of Mount Everest.
   a. sweets and a camera
   b. a cross and a flag
   c. sweets and a cross
   d. a flag and sweets

Word root: eu

1. **euphoria** = eu (good) + phoria (feeling)
   eulogy = eu (good) + logy (word)
   euphony = eu (good) + phony (sound)

2. **euphoria:** good, feeling → a feeling of happiness
   eulogy: good, word → praise of a dead person
   euphony: good, sound → a pleasant sound

3. Complete the following sentences choosing the right word.

   | euphoria | eulogy | euphony |

   a. I gave a _____ at my father's funeral.

   b. The orchestra produced _____.

   c. After I won the lottery, I had a feel of _____.

Reading comprehension II

Inference and purpose

It can be inferred from the passage that _____ .

   a. Edmund Hillary spent most of his life near Mount Everest

   b. John Hunt made it to the top of Mount Everest

   c. Tenzing Norgay spent most of his life near Mount Everest

   d. John Hunt spent most of his life near Mount Everest

Coherence

Look at the four squares [■] that indicate where the following sentence can be added to the passage below. Where would the sentence best fit?

Hillary's list of accomplishments makes him one of the great explorers and mountain climbers of all time.

■ Following the first successful ascent of Everest, Hillary continued mountain climbing and exploring. ■ He climbed ten other peaks in the Himalayas. In 1958 he was part of an expedition to the South Pole, and in 1985 he accompanied Neil Armstrong, the first man to step on the moon, in a flight over the Arctic Ocean to the North Pole, becoming the first man to stand on both poles and the top of the world. ■ Tenzing Norgay became the director of the Himalayan Mountaineering Institute and continued to climb in the Himalayas. ■

Listening comprehension

Main idea

What is the lecture mainly about?

    a. The relationship between Nepal and Tibet

    b. The lowest point on Earth

    c. George Mallory and Andrew Irvine

    d. Many attempts to climb Mount Everest

Details

1. What is true about Mount Everest?

    a. Only 20 people were killed on the mountain.

    b. More than 3,000 people have succeeded in climbing the mountain.

    c. George Mallory successfully climbed the mountain.

    d. It is 29,029 feet high.

2. What is true about Hillary and Norgay?

    a. They were the first to discover Mount Everest.

    b. They successfully climbed Mount Everest.

    c. They were famous photographers.

    d. They were killed on Mount Everest.

Paraphrasing

Mount Everest is located on the border of Nepal and Tibet, China.

Which of the sentences below best expresses the essential information in the highlighted sentence in the passage? Incorrect choices change the meaning in important ways or leave out essential information.

    a. Mount Everest is the border between Nepal and Tibet, China.

    b. Mount Everest sits in Nepal near Tibet, China.

    c. On the border between Nepal and Tibet, China sits Mount Everest.

    d. The border between Nepal and Tibet, China is near Mount Everest.

Summary

Complete the following list by choosing the three true sentences about the passage.

-
-
-

a. Mount Everest is the second highest mountain in the world.

b. Mount Everest was first climbed in 1953.

c. Sir Edmund Hillary was born in New Zealand.

d. No one has climbed Mount Everest since Hillary and Norgay.

e. People who die on Mount Everest are buried in a special cemetery in Nepal.

f. Edmund Hillary stood on the North Pole and the South Pole.

Speaking

What qualities do you value in a friend?

Model response

1. Fill in the blanks using the words in the box.

> understand   negative   value   good   honesty   wrong

The qualities I _____ most in my friends are _____ and understanding. I think a truly _____ friend will always be honest with you, even when it is difficult to tell the truth. My best friends will tell me when I'm _____. I might get upset with them at the time, but I know that they are telling me the truth because they are my friends. Also my good friends _____ me and accept my good and bad qualities. It is nice to have friends who know my _____ traits and still like me.

2. Using your own words, answer the question above. Then talk to the class.

Harriet Tubman

Pre-reading activity

1. Was there ever slavery in your country?
2. What do you think the Underground Railroad could be?
3. Is there still slavery anywhere in the world?

1 Harriet Tubman was born into slavery in 1820 in the state of **Maryland**, U.S.A. Originally named Araminta, she later changed her name because her given name reminded her of slavery. Growing up as a slave, Harriet had to do physically demanding work. Because she was unusually strong, she was hired out to other farms to do chores, such as split wood, drive oxen, and haul logs. Being a slave, she was not allowed to attend school and never obtained a formal education, but she had an innate intelligence that served her well. During her childhood, she sustained a serious injury and nearly died when an angry overseer threw a two-pound metal weight at her, striking her in the forehead. Although she recovered from her injuries, she had an ugly scar on her forehead and suffered from seizures the rest of her life. These lasting injuries served to remind her of the cruelty of slavery.

2 In 1849, her master died and she learned that she was to be sold to another family in the Deep South. She was determined not to let this happen. With her two brothers, she escaped and headed north to freedom. She used the North Star to guide her and received help from the Underground Railroad, a series of safe houses set up to help escaped slaves reach freedom in the North. Once free, Harriet could not rest while so many others remained enslaved.

....

Maryland   a state north of Washington D.C. and
              south of New Jersey in the United
              States
courage   bravery

Civil War   a war fought in the 19th century over
               the issue of slavery between the
               northern and southern states of the
               United States

3 She was determined to help as many slaves escape as she could, so she became a conductor on the Underground Railroad. This meant that she would help to guide other escaped slaves to freedom. For the next ten years, she made over twenty trips back into the South and helped over 300 slaves to freedom. This was extremely dangerous. If she were captured, she would either be returned to slavery or killed. While in the North, she worked as a cook or dressmaker to earn money to help support the freed slaves until they could find work. In 1857, she bravely returned to the South and freed both of her aged parents. Harriet's work gained her a reputation in the North and the South. In the North she was loved and respected for her **courage** and dedication; in the South she was hated.

4 When the **Civil War** broke out, Harriet immediately joined the fight. She volunteered to help the **Union Army** and served as a scout, spy, nurse, and cook. When the war ended, she continued her work to help African Americans by working tirelessly to establish schools and hospitals.

5 With the help of her friend, Sarah Hopkins Bradford, Harriet wrote a book about her life titled "Scenes in the Life of Harriet Tubman." With the money earned from this book, she was able to buy a house and settle down with her husband, Nelson Davis, a black Civil War veteran. In her later years, she continued to work for African American rights and women's rights. On March 10, 1913, Harriet died of **pneumonia**. She was buried with full military honors. There are several memorials erected to honor the life of this amazing woman, but the biggest honor was bestowed on February 1, 1978. On this date the Harriet Tubman **stamp** was issued in her memory, the first stamp to honor an African American.

Union Army the army of the northern states during the Civil War
pneumonia a disease marked by inflammation of the lungs with congestion

stamp a small adhesive token issued by the government to be stuck on mail to indicate that postage has been paid

Vocabulary Study I

Match the word with its synonym.

1. chore
2. demanding
3. escape
4. guide
5. establish

a. institute
b. arduous
c. steer
d. routine
e. abscond

Reading comprehension I

Main idea

1. What's the passage about?
   a. Slavery
   b. The Underground Railroad
   c. Harriet Tubman
   d. The Civil War

Detail questions

1. Harriet Tubman was born _____.
   a. Julie
   b. Sarah
   c. Araminta
   d. Mary

2. Harriet Tubman was helped by _____ on her way to freedom.
   a. Abraham Lincoln
   b. the Underground Railroad
   c. the Union Army
   d. Sarah Hopkins Bradford

3. Harriet Tubman married _____.
   a. Nelson Davis
   b. Fredrick Douglas
   c. Joseph Tubman
   d. Charles Truman

Vocabulary Study II

Word root: auto

1. **autobiography =** auto (self) + bio (life) + graphy (write)
   autograph = auto (self) + graph (write)
   automatic = auto (self) + matic (thinking, movement)

2. **autobiography:** self, life, write → a person's life story written by the person
   autograph: self, write → a person's own signature
   automatic: self, thinking, movement → operating on its own

3. Complete the following sentences choosing the right word.

autobiographies	autographs	automatic

   a. Blinking is an _____ response to bright lights.

   b. My favorite books are _____ about famous movie stars.

   c. I collect _____ of famous people.

Reading comprehension II

Inference and purpose

It can be inferred form the passage that Harriet Tubman _____ .

   a. is a respected person in American history   b. died in the Civil War

   c. became President   d. was very wealthy

Coherence

Look at the four squares [■] that indicate where the following sentence can be added to the passage below. Where would the sentence best fit?

On every trip to the South there was a chance of being caught.

■ She was determined to help as many slaves escape as she could, so she became a conductor on the Underground Railroad. ■ This meant that she would help to guide other escaped slaves to freedom. For the next ten years she made over twenty trips back into the South and helped over 300 slaves to freedom. This was extremely dangerous. ■ If she were captured, she would either be returned to slavery or killed. While in the North she worked as a cook or dressmaker to earn money to help support the freed slaves until they could find work. ■ In 1857, she bravely returned to the South and freed both of her aged parents.

Listening comprehension

Main idea

What is the lecture mainly about?

  a. Harriet's career as a dressmaker

  b. Harriet's aged parents

  c. Harriet's life as a savior of slaves

  d. The Underground Railroad

Details

1. What is true about Harriet?

  a. She hated black slaves so much.

  b. She ran a train company.

  c. She helped many black slaves.

  d. She helped only 30 slaves.

2. What is true about the Underground Railroad?

  a. It was a famous subway station.

  b. Actually, it was a bus company.

  c. It helped escaped slaves.

  d. Only black people could work for the company.

Paraphrasing

When the Civil War broke out, Harriet immediately joined the fight.

Which of the sentences below best expresses the essential information in the highlighted sentence in the passage? Incorrect choices change the meaning in important ways or leave out essential information.

  a. Harriet fought in the Civil War.

  b. Harriet was fighting when the Civil War broke out.

  c. Harriet joined the army at the start of the Civil War.

  d. Harriet couldn't fight because she was an African American.

Summary

Complete the following list by choosing the three true sentences about the passage.

-
-
-

a. Harriet Tubman was born a slave.

b. Harriet was born in New York City.

c. Harriet escaped to freedom.

d. Harriet became President of the United States.

e. With the help of a friend, Harriet wrote a book about her life

f. Harriet established the Underground Railroad.

Speaking

Who do you think is brave?

Model response

1. Fill in the blanks using the words in the box.

> first   never   speak   overcome   control   practice

I don't think people who do things and are _____ scared are brave; I think the really brave people are the ones who are scared but _____ their fear. I was really brave once. When I was _____ learning English, I was really scared to _____ in class. I was afraid everyone would laugh at me, but I knew I would never get any better if I didn't _____. One day in class I decided I wasn't going to let my fears _____ me. I volunteered to speak in class. I made some mistakes, but no one laughed, and I got better. That was the bravest I've ever been.

2. Using your own words, answer the question above. Then talk to the class.

UFOs

Pre-reading activity
1. Have you ever seen something you couldn't explain?
2. Do you believe in life on other planets?
3. Do you think aliens have visited Earth?

1 Invaders from outer space, little green men, flying saucers — do you believe in any or all of these? People from all over the world have reported seeing unidentified flying objects, or UFOs. Despite all of these sightings, no one has been able to explain what UFOs are. Some UFOs can easily be explained as **weather balloons** or by unusual weather phenomena, but there are other sights that seem to defy any easy explanation. The first widely publicized UFO sighting was in 1947. A private businessman flying his private plane near Mount Rainer, **Washington**, reported seeing nine bright objects flying across the sky at an incredible speed. He described the objects as disks moving across the sky like a saucer being skipped over water. This gave rise to the term "flying saucer." Since this sighting, there have been tens of thousands of sightings, but reported sightings of unexplained flying objects have occurred throughout human history.

2 It is difficult to interpret ancient reports of flying objects, and many of these reports were undoubtedly natural phenomena, but some historical reports are difficult to explain. On September 24, 1235, **General** Kujo Yoritsume and his army observed globes of light flying in the night sky near Kyoto, Japan. The General's **advisors** told him not to worry, that it was just the wind moving the stars. Three centuries later and a continent away, there was another unexplained sighting. On April 14, 1561, in the skies over Nuremberg,

---

weather balloon a balloon that carries instruments used to make measurements about the weather

Washington a state in the northwestern part of the United States north of Oregon and west of Montana

Germany, numerous people reported seeing a multitude of flying objects that seemed to be engaged in an aerial battle. The reports said that smaller spheres and disks emerged from larger cylinders. These eyewitness accounts are difficult to explain because there were so many witnesses and no obvious explanation. Further evidence of UFOs comes from the art world. Art historians have long noted that many works of art from past centuries show objects in the backgrounds that are remarkably similar to modern UFO sightings.

3 The first modern UFO sighting occurred in Copiapo City, **Chile**, in July, 1868. Since then, there have been multiple unexplained accounts of flying objects and many of these accounts have had numerous witnesses. Sightings tend to come in waves. In the 1880s, reports of mystery airships appeared in American newspapers. Between 1909 and 1912, sightings of similar aircraft were reported in the U.S.A., Europe, and New Zealand. During World War II, pilots in Europe and the Pacific reported balls of light or spheres that followed aircrafts. On February 25, 1942, the U.S. military both visually and on radar identified a UFO over **Los Angeles**. The UFO was shot at for twenty minutes but continued to fly. Like so many other incidents, this UFO remains a mystery.

4 The U.S. Air Force studied UFO sightings from 1947 to 1970. The report said that most sightings were due to misidentification, some were hoaxes, and others remain unexplained. Several U.S. government studies have concluded that 22 to 33 percent of UFO sightings are unexplained. Despite the number of unexplained sightings, the majority of scientists believe that all UFOs are due to some ordinary phenomena. Regardless of what the scientists think, the most popular explanation for UFOs is that we have been visited from other worlds.

---

advisor an expert who gives advice
general the highest rank for an army officer
Chile a country in southern South America

Los Angeles a city in the southern part of the state of California

Vocabulary Study I

Match the word with its synonym.

1. invader	a. identical
2. saucer	b. baffling
3. unexplained	c. dish
4. similar	d. intruder
5. sphere	e. orb

Reading comprehension I

Main idea

What's the passage about?

a. Unidentified flying objects   b. spaceships

c. Planes   d. World War II

Detail questions

1. General Yoritsumi's advisors told him the globes of light were _____.

   a. spaceships

   b. moons pushed by the wind

   c. stars being pushed by the wind

   d. a new enemy weapon

2. The first modern UFO sighting occurred in _____.

   a. Germany   b. Japan

   c. Chile   d. America

3. The spheres seen over Nuremberg, Germany, seemed to be _____.

   a. bring food   b. transporting people

   c. doing battle   d. taking pictures

Vocabulary Study II

Word root: od, odus

1. **period =** peri (around) + od (way)
    method = meth (after) + od (way)
    exodus = ex (out) + odus (way) +

2. **period:** around, way → recurring cycle of time
    method: seek, way → a way of doing something
    exodus: out, way → a group leaving

3. Complete the following sentences choosing the right word.

periods	method	exodus

    a. He developed a better _____ to catch mice.

    b. The Olympic Games are held in four year _____.

    c. During the famine the people made an _____ out of the country.

Reading comprehension II

Inference and purpose

It can be inferred from the passage that _____ .

   a. thousands of people have seen UFOs
   b. UFOs are from Mars
   c. people who see UFOs have bad eye sight
   d. the Japanese report seeing the most UFOs

Coherence

Look at the four squares [■] that indicate where the following sentence can be added to the passage below. Where would the sentence best fit?

> **Many people believe that creatures from other worlds have visited the Earth for years.**

■ Invaders from outer space, little green men, flying saucers — do you believe in any or all of these? ■ People from all over the world have reported seeing Unidentified flying objects, or UFOs. ■ Despite all of these sightings, no one has been able to explain what UFOs are. Some UFOs can easily be explained as weather balloons or by unusual weather phenomena, but there are other sights that seem to defy any easy explanation. ■ The first widely publicized UFO sighting was in 1947.

Listening comprehension

Main idea

What is the lecture mainly about?

    a. General Kujo Yoritsume's private life

    b. The beauty of natural phenomena

    c. The importance of interpretation in ancient society

    d. Reports of unidentified flying objects

Details

1. What is true about the year of 1235?

    a. In that year, many flying objects fought with each other.

    b. In that year, Japan fought with America.

    c. In that year, some soldiers saw some light near Kyoto.

    d. In that year, Martians invaded the Earth.

2. What is true about the year of 1561?

    a. In that year, people saw flying objects near Kyoto.

    b. In that year, some people fought against flying objects.

    c. In that year, some people watched flying objects.

    d. In that year, General Yoritsume invaded America.

Paraphrasing

Invaders for outer space, little green men, flying saucers — do you believe in any or all of these?

Which of the sentences below best expresses the essential information in the highlighted sentence in the passage? Incorrect choices change the meaning in important ways or leave out essential information.

    a. Do little green men believe in you?

    b. Do little green men fly flying saucers?

    c. Do you believe in invaders from outer space, little green men, or flying saucers?

    d. The invaders from outer space are little green men who arrive in flying saucers.

Summary

Complete the following list by choosing the three true sentences about the passage.

-
-
-

a. The first UFO sighting was in 1947.

b. No one has been able to explain all UFO sightings.

c. Art historians have described unexplained objects in the skies of ancient paintings.

d. In 1561 pilots over Nuremberg, Germany reported seeing UFOs.

e. The US Air Force claimed to have explained all UFO sightings.

f. UFO sightings tend to come in waves.

Speaking

What is the hardest part about learning a new language?

Model response

1. Fill in the blanks using the words in the box.

them	English	times	language	pretty	frustrated

   For me, the hardest part about learning a new _____ is not being able to say what I want to say. I've been studying _____ for a long time, and I think my English is getting _____ good. But there are still _____ when I can't think of the right words to say what I want to. Even though I get _____, people always try to help me and eventually I'm able to make _____ understand my meaning.

2. Using your own words, answer the question above. Then talk to the class.

The Space Race

Pre-reading activity

1. Have you ever thought of traveling in space?
2. Why did people go to space?
3. Who was the first person in space?

1 The space race was a competition between the United States and the Soviet Union to see who could explore space first. This competition was born out of the cultural, technological, and **ideological** rivalry between these two countries. Following World War II, the U.S.A. and the **U.S.S.R.** were the dominant powers in the world, each representing opposing ideologies: the U.S.A. was a **capitalist** country, while the USSR was a **communist** one. During this period these two superpowers, as they came to be known, each tried to show that their ideology was superior to the other's. The space race was just one aspect of this rivalry.

2 The space race was launched on October 4th, 1957, when the U.S.S.R. sent Sputnik 1, the first manmade satellite, into orbit around the Earth. The people in both countries were distrustful of each other. Many Americans were fearful that Sputnik might be some kind of new weapon. It also created insecurity in the American public. Before the Sputnik launch, most Americans believed that their country was superior technologically to the Soviets. The Sputnik launch spurred the American people and government into action. The government passed a bill giving more than a billion dollars to help educate promising students in the sciences. Following the Sputnik launch, the Americans had several embarrassing launch failures, but four months after Sputnik, the Americans successfully launched Explorer 1.

ideological   referring to the body of ideas that describe the social needs and aspirations of an individual, group, or society

U.S.S.R.   Union of Soviet Socialist Republics, a union between Russia and several other Soviet republics, including Ukraine and Belorussia, which ceased to exist on December 31, 1991

3 The two hostile nations competed to make firsts in space. The Americans sent fruit flies into space to be the first to send living creatures into space; the Soviets sent two dogs in an orbit around the Earth. The next big prize was to see who could put a man in space first. The Soviets sent Yuri Gagarin into orbit around the Earth on April 12, 1961, creating **headlines** around the world. Twenty-three days later, Alan Shepard of America entered space. The next target was landing a man on the moon.

4 Luna was the Soviet program designed to explore the moon and test technology that would, if successful, ultimately send a man to the moon. The equivalent program for the Americans was the Pioneer program. The early successes by the Soviets prompted the then U.S. president, President Kennedy, to make his famous promise that the U.S.A. would land a man on the moon and return him safely to Earth by the end of the decade. At the time, this seemed like a fantastic, almost impossible, feat. After Kennedy's promise, the Apollo program was launched. The Soviets were **reluctant** to pursue a moon mission, partly because of the potential of defeat, but also because of the huge financial costs of such a program. A year after Kennedy made his promise, the Soviets committed themselves to attempting a moon mission.

5 On July 21, 1969, Neil Armstrong fulfilled Kennedy's promise and became the first human to walk on the moon. Over 500 million people from around the world watched and listened as Neil Armstrong made his historic first steps on the moon's surface. As he stepped on the moon's surface, Armstrong made what is now a famous comment "That's one small step for man, one giant leap for mankind." The space race began as a rivalry between two powerful countries, but in the end, as Armstrong's words say, the accomplishments were for all of us.

---

capitalist   refers to an economic system based on private ownership of capital

communist   refers to an economic system based on government ownership of capital

headline   the title of a newspaper article, usually set in large type

reluctant   unwilling

Vocabulary Study I

Match the word with its synonym.

1. explore
2. superior
3. fearful
4. impossible
5. feat

a. apprehensive
b. unfeasible
c. investigate
d. accomplishment
e. enhanced

Reading comprehension I

Main idea

What's the passage about?

a. The ideology of the U.S.A. and the U.S.S.R.
b. The rivalry between the U.S.A. and the U.S.S.R.
c. The race to space between the U.S.A. and the U.S.S.R.
d. Racing in the Olympics.

Detail questions

1. Sputnik was launched in _____.
   a. 1947   b. 1957
   c. 1967   d. 1969

2. The first living things in space were _____.
   a. monkeys   b. dogs
   c. fruit flies   d. cats

3. Who said, "That's one small step for man, one giant leap for mankind"?
   a. President Kennedy   b. Neil Armstrong
   c. Yuri Gagarin   d. Alan Shepard

Vocabulary Study II

Word root: aqua

1. **aquaduct =** aqua (water) + duct (lead)
   aqualung = aqua (water) **+ lung** (the light organ)
   aquamarine = aqua (water) **+ marine** (sea)

2. **aquaduct:** water, lead → conduit built to carry running water
   aqualung: water, light organ → device that allows breathing under water
   aquamarine: water, sea → blue-green color

3. Complete the following sentences choosing the right word.

aquaducts	aqualung	aquamarine

   a. The Romans built many _____ to supply their cities with water.

   b. The car is an _____ color.

   c. The diver uses an _____ to help him study fish.

Reading comprehension II

Inference and purpose

The purpose of the passage was to inform the reader about _____ .

   a. the ideologies of the Soviet Union and the U.S.A.   b. communism

   c. the race to space   d. capitalism

Coherence

Look at the four squares [■] that indicate where the following sentence can be added to the passage below. Where would the sentence best fit?

The Americans were still behind in the race for space, but not for long.

■ The two hostile nations competed to make firsts in space. The Americans sent fruit flies into space to be the first to send living creatures into space; the Soviets sent two dogs in an orbit around the Earth. ■ The next big prize was to see who could put a man in space first. ■ The Soviets sent Yuri Gagarin into orbit around the Earth on April 12, 1961, creating headlines around the world. ■ Twenty-three days later, Alan Shepard of America entered space.

Listening comprehension

Main idea

What is the lecture mainly about?

 a. The arms race between the U.S.A. and the U.S.S.R.
 b. The space race between the U.S.A. and the U.S.S.R.
 c. New kinds of weapons
 d. The first artificial satellite

Details

1. What is true about Sputnik 1?
 a. It was the first artificial satellite.
 b. It landed on the moon.
 c. Americans believed that it would be used peacefully.
 d. The U.S.A. launched it.

2. What is true about Explorer 1?
 a. It was a new kind of weapon.
 b. It was the first manmade satellite.
 c. The U.S.A. launched it.
 d. Russians failed to attack the satellite.

Paraphrasing

During this period these two superpowers, as they came to be known, each tried to show that their ideology was superior to the other's.

Which of the sentences below best expresses the essential information in the highlighted sentence in the passage? Incorrect choices change the meaning in important ways or leave out essential information.

 a. The two most powerful countries in the world each had a superior ideology than the other.
 b. The world's two superpowers shared the same ideology and each wanted win the race to space.
 c. The ideologies of the two most powerful nations were superior to all of the other ideologies.
 d. The two most powerful nations on Earth tried to show that their ideology was better than the other's.

Summary

Complete the following list by choosing the three true sentences about the passage.

-
-
-

a. The U.S.A. launched Sputnik in 1957.

b. Alan Shepard was the first person into space.

c. Neil Armstrong was the first person to walk on the moon.

d. Sputnik was the first manmade satellite into orbit.

e. Yuri Gagarin was the first man to walk on the moon.

f. The U.S.A. and the U.S.S.R. raced to be the first to reach space.

Speaking

What is your biggest dream?

Model response

1. Fill in the blanks using the words in the box.

> experience   think   dream   space   pictures   gravity

My biggest _____ is to travel in space. I love looking at _____ of the Earth taken from _____, and someday I want to look at the Earth from space myself. I _____ it would be fun to try to spot my country from thousands of miles above. In space there is no _____, so I wouldn't weigh anything. It would be fun to float in the air. I think going to space would be a great _____.

2. Using your own words, answer the question above. Then talk to the class.

Queen Victoria

Pre-reading activity

1. Does your country have a king or queen?
2. Who is the most famous king or queen?
3. Have you heard of Queen Victoria?

1 Queen Victoria was born Alexandrina Victoria on May 24, 1819. She would go on to become the longest reigning British **monarch** in history. She took the throne on June 20, 1837, and held it until her death, sixty-three years later, on January 22, 1901. Her reign took place at the height of the Industrial Revolution and a period of great economic and technological growth in **Great Britain**. This period has become known as the Victorian era — an era that saw tremendous expansion of the British **Empire**, making it the undisputed foremost global power.

2 Alexandrina Victoria's father died of pneumonia eight months after her birth and her grandfather died six days later. Her mother began to prepare her for the possibility of ascending to the throne one day. As a child, she was taught German, English, Italian, Latin, Chinese, and French. Her favorite subject was history. The reigning King William IV had no children, so young Alexandrina became heiress presumptive, meaning that she would become queen upon the King's death. King William IV died of a heart attack four weeks after Alexandrina's eighteenth birthday. Princess Alexandrina was now Queen Victoria.

3 The Princess met her future husband, Prince Albert, when she was just sixteen years old. It was three years later when they met again that romance began. Being the Queen, she had to propose. The couple was married on February 10,

---

monarch a hereditary sovereign as a king, queen, or emperor etc.
Great Britain referring to England, Scotland, and Wales

empire a political unit that comprises of a number of territories or nations ruled by a single supreme authority

1840. By all accounts they had a happy marriage. The couple's first of nine children was born on November 21, 1840. Prince Albert not only became her companion but also her most trusted advisor.

4 During the Queen's long reign there were multiple attempts on her life. In 1840, while she was **pregnant** with her first child, Edward Oxford fired two shots at the Queen while she was riding with her husband. No one was injured in this incident. Oxford was tried for high **treason** but was **acquitted** by reason of insanity. In 1842, two more men fired shots at the Queen. She was not injured in either incident. In 1849, a man fired at the Queen's carriage as it passed and again the Queen was uninjured. In 1850, a possibly insane ex-army officer struck the Queen with his gun, causing some bruising. Despite these attempts on her life, the Queen was an extremely popular monarch.

5 Prince Albert died of typhoid fever in 1861. Queen Victoria was devastated by the loss. She went into a state of mourning and wore black the rest of her life. Following Albert's death, she rarely visited London and remained secluded. Her seclusion earned her the nickname "the Widow of Windsor."

6 Queen Victoria's rule saw the evolution of a modern constitutional monarchy. The royal family's role became more symbolic. Victoria placed a strong emphasis on moral and family values, making the monarchy something the middle class could identify with. She was a major figure internationally, both as a symbol of the British Empire and through her family lines that ran through many of the royal families of Europe. Many of the current European monarchs can trace their family lines back to Queen Victoria. In 2002, the BBC conducted a poll to choose the 100 greatest Britons in history. Queen Victoria was number eighteen.

---

pregnant having a child developing in the body   **acquit** to declare not guilty
treason betrayal to one's country

Vocabulary Study I

Match the word with its synonym.

1. monarch	a. ruler
2. presumptive	b. infection
3. identify	c. ascertain
4. advisor	d. ostensible
5. fever	e. counselor

Reading comprehension I

Main idea

What's the passage about?

a. The British monarchy   b. Attempts to kill the Queen

c. The life of Queen Victoria   d. Great Britain

Detail questions

1. Queen Victoria was _____.

   a. the first queen of Great Britain

   b. the last queen of Great Britain

   c. killed by a gun shot

   d. the longest reigning queen in British history

2. Prince Albert died of _____.

   a. typhoid fever   b. a gun shot

   c. pneumonia   d. old age

3. Victoria became queen when _____ died.

   a. King George IV   b. King Henry VIII

   c. King William IV   d. Queen Elizabeth II

Vocabulary Study II

Word root: neo

1. **neologism** = neo (new) + logism (word)
   neonate = neo (new) + nate (born)
   neophyte = neo (new) + phyte (planet)

2. **neologism:** new, word → a new word or expression
   neonate: new, born → recently born infant
   neophyte: new, planet → a person who is new to a subject

3. Complete the following sentences choosing the right word.

neologisms	neonate	neophyte

   a. Young people often create _____ that are unique to their generation.

   b. I'm a _____ at Spanish; I can't speak a word.

   c. Someone in the first few weeks of life is called a _____.

Reading comprehension II

Inference and purpose

It can be inferred from this passage that _____ .

   a. Queen Victoria was an important figure in British history

   b. Prince Albert later became king

   c. Queen Victoria has been forgotten by most of the British people

   d. Queen Victoria had no children

Coherence

Look at the four squares [■] that indicate where the following sentence can be added to the passage below. Where would the sentence best fit?

This left a hole in Alexandrina's life that her mother tried to fill.

■ Alexandrina Victoria's father died of pneumonia eight months after her birth and her grandfather died six days later. ■ Her mother began to prepare her for the possibility of ascending to the throne one day. ■ As a child, she was taught German, English, Italian, Latin, Chinese, and French. Her favorite subject was history. ■ The reigning King William IV had no children, so young Alexandrina became heiress presumptive, meaning that she would become queen upon the King's death.

Listening comprehension

Main idea

What is the lecture mainly about?

    a. The tragic death of Alexandrina's grandmother

    b. How Princess Alexandrina became queen

    c. How England became the most powerful country

    d. Why Princess Alexandrina learned foreign languages

Details

1. What is true about Princess Alexandrina?

    a. She had no children.

    b. She got married at age thirteen.

    c. She was Italian.

    d. She learned Chinese.

2. What is true about King William IV?

    a. He lived to be ninety.   b. He had eight children.

    c. He died of a heart attack.   d. He was French.

Paraphrasing

> **Her reign took place at the height of the Industrial Revolution and a period of great economic and technological growth in Great Britain.**

Which of the sentences below best expresses the essential information in the highlighted sentence in the passage? Incorrect choices change the meaning in important ways or leave out essential information.

    a. Great Britain enjoyed great industrial, economic, and technological growth during her reign.

    b. She created great industrial, economic, and technological growth during her reign.

    c. Queen Victoria brought about the Industrial Revolution and with it great economic and technological growth

    d. The economy of Great Britain grew during her reign.

Summary

Complete the following list by choosing the three true sentences about the passage.

-
-
-

a. Queen Victoria was the shortest reigning monarch in British history.

b. Queen Victoria was born in 1919.

c. Edward Oxford became King after Queen Victoria died.

d. Queen Victoria was the longest reigning monarch in British history.

e. Queen Victoria married Prince Albert

f. There were several attempts on Queen Victoria's life.

Speaking

What is your favorite holiday in your country and why?

Model response

1. Fill in the blanks using the words in the box.

   | what   dress up   months   holiday   great   somebody |

   I'm from America, and my favorite American _____ is Halloween. I love Halloween because I get to _____ in a costume and be _____ or something else for a night. Every year a few _____ before Halloween, my friends and I start thinking of _____ we'll dress up as for Halloween. Last year I dressed up as a vampire; this year I think I'll be a rockstar. I always have a _____ time on Halloween.

2. Using your own words, answer the question above. Then talk to the class.

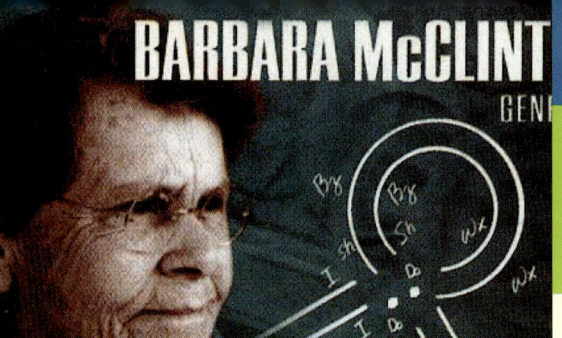

Barbara McClintock

Pre-reading activity
1. What makes you look the way you do?
2. Have you heard of genetics?
3. Who is the greatest geneticist of the twentieth century?

1 In the first half of the twentieth century, there were many **obstacles** to a woman pursuing a career in science. Many people felt that science was an area of study where only men could excel. If a woman showed a natural talent in mathematics or science, she would probably be discouraged from developing her talents. That is what makes the career of Barbara McClintock all the more remarkable. Many of her male colleagues found McClintock's independence, originality, and brilliance intimidating. In one well-known example, her advisor became irritated with her when she solved a problem that he had been working on for most of his professional life. She eventually had to leave the research team. McClintock began her career in science in 1919 at **Cornell University**, and despite tremendous social pressure and adversity, she is now seen as one of the top scientists of the century.

2 McClintock was born in Hartford, **Connecticut**, in 1902. Her father was a physician while her mother was a housewife. As a child, she was described as being independent and a bit of a tomboy. She learned science in high school and wanted to pursue her studies at Cornell University. Her mother didn't want her to attend a university because she thought it would make her unmarriageable. She almost wasn't allowed to attend college, but her father intervened.

....

obstacle something that obstructs or hinders progress

Cornell University one of the Ivy League universities in the United States located in Ithaca, New York

3 While at Cornell, she studied botany and received her BSc in 1923. As an undergraduate, she took her first course in genetics, a course taught by C.B. Hutchison. Hutchison was so impressed by McClintock's interest that he invited her to attend a graduate seminar on genetics. McClintock later pointed to that invitation as the reason she pursued a career in genetics. She went on to earn a PhD in botany and became an instructor in the department.

4 McClintock made many contributions to the field of plant genetics. One of her colleagues noted that McClintock had made 10 out of 17 significant contributions in the field of genetics made by Cornell scientists between 1929 and 1935. Years later, while working at the Cold Spring Harbor Research Institute, she made her most surprising discovery. By studying the color patterns on maze, she found that genes were controlled by activator genes that could change position or "jump." This **countered** everything geneticists believed at the time. When she presented her papers, she was met with puzzlement or even **hostility**. Although she knew she was right, she stopped publishing her research in 1953 because other scientists were unable to understand it. She went into semi-retirement — just teaching graduate students and conducting research.

5 Two decades later, with the introduction of new technology, scientists rediscovered McClintock's research and found it to be correct. Over thirty years after she originally presented her research findings, Barbara McClintock was awarded the **Nobel Prize** in Physiology and Medicine. To this day, she is still the only woman to receive an unshared Nobel Prize in this field. Barbara McClintock was always ahead of her time. As a student she studied science when women weren't supposed to, and then as a scientist she made discoveries that her peers couldn't understand for decades.

....

Connecticut   a state in the northeastern part of the United States
counter   to go against, defy
hostility   unfriendliness, antagonism

Nobel Prize   an award established by Alfred B. Nobel in 1901 for outstanding achievement in chemistry, physics, medicine or physiology, literature, and the promotion of peace

Vocabulary Study I

Match the word with its synonym.

1. excel   a. chase
2. tremendous   b. confusion
3. pursue   c. surpass
4. puzzlement   d. terrific
5. unshared   e. alone

Reading comprehension I

Main idea

What's the passage about?

a. The achievements of Barbara McClintock
b. Genetics
c. Corn
d. The research done at Cornell University

Detail questions

1. McClintock learned science in _____.
   a. the library   b. books
   c. the park   d. high school

2. When McClintock first presented her ideas on activator genes, other scientists were _____.
   a. excited   b. surprised and excited
   c. confused   d. bored

3. Two decades after McClintock's discoveries, her research was proved to be _____.
   a. wrong   b. partially wrong
   c. partially right   d. correct

Vocabulary Study II

Word root: mit, mess

1. **permission =** per (through) + miss (send) + ion (noun forming)

    submit = sub (under) + miss (send)

    emit = e (out) + mit (send)

2. **permission:** through, send, noun → giving consent

    submission: under, send → giving control to another

    emit: out, send → to give off or out

3. Complete the following sentences choosing the right word.

    > permission   submitted   emitted

    a. The factory _____ a bad smell

    b. He _____ the report to his teacher for grading.

    c. You must ask the King for _____ to enter.

Reading comprehension II

Inference and purpose

It can be inferred from this passage that Barbara McClintock was very _____ .

    a. intelligent   b. lucky

    c. athletic   d. fun

Coherence

Look at the four squares [■] that indicate where the following sentence can be added to the passage below. Where would the sentence best fit?

> **This was a long wait but Barbara McClintock's conviction in her groundbreaking research was finally vindicated.**

■ Two decades later, with the introduction of new technology, scientists rediscovered McClintock's research and found it to be correct. Over thirty years after she originally presented her research findings, Barbara McClintock was awarded the Nobel Prize in Physiology and Medicine. ■ To this day, she is still the only woman to receive an unshared Nobel Prize in this field. Barbara McClintock was always ahead of her time. ■ As a student she studied science when women weren't supposed to, and then as a scientist she made discoveries that her peers couldn't understand for decades. ■

Listening comprehension

Main idea

What is the lecture mainly about?

    a. McClintock's genius as a musician

    b. McClintock's fame and wealth

    c. McClintock's career as a grammarian

    d. McClintock's contribution to genetics

Details

1. What is true about McClintock?

    a. She was an ordinary geneticist.

    b. Most scientists welcomed her new discovery.

    c. She made genetically modified crops.

    d. She made significant contributions to genetics.

2. What is true about activator genes?

    a. They could not change position.

    b. Most geneticists were aware of their existence.

    c. They were discovered by McClintock

    d. They were controlled by ordinary genes.

Paraphrasing

> **Two decades later, with the introduction of new technology, scientists rediscovered McClintock's research and found it to be correct.**

Which of the sentences below best expresses the essential information in the highlighted sentence in the passage? Incorrect choices change the meaning in important ways or leave out essential information.

    a. With the help of new technology, scientists rediscovered McClintock's research after two decades and discovered she was right.

    b. McClintock rediscovered her research after two decades, and using new technologies proved to other scientists that she was right.

    c. Two decades after McClintock conducted her research, she used new technologies to prove that she was correct.

    d. Two decades after McClintock conducted her research, scientists used new technologies to prove that she had made a mistake.

Summary

Complete the following list by choosing the three true sentences about the passage.

-
-
-

a. Barbara McClintock never earned credit for work.

b. Barbara McClintock went to Cornell University.

c. Barbara McClintock was born in England.

d. Barbara McClintock studied maze.

e. Barbara McClintock went to Harvard University.

f. Barbara McClintock won the Nobel Prize.

Speaking

If you could do anything, what would you most want to do?

Model response

1. Fill in the blanks using the words in the box.

two   player   anything   country   greatest   dream

If I could do_____, I would be the greatest soccer _____ in the world. I love to play soccer, and if I was the best player, I could help my _____ win the World Cup. My _____ has always been to see my country win the World Cup. This way two of my biggest dreams would come true. I would be the world's _____ soccer player, and my country would win the World Cup. That would be _____ dreams come true.

2. Using your own words, answer the question above. Then talk to the class.

Rocks

Pre-reading activity

1. What is the Earth made of?
2. How are rocks made?
3. Are all rocks made the same way?

1 When an average person looks at a rock, this is all they can tell you: it's a rock. When a geologist looks at a rock, you might hear something very different. A geologist can look at a rock and tell you its history and how and where it was formed. There are three basic types of rocks on the Earth: igneous, sedimentary, and metamorphic. Each type was formed in a different way and has a different history.

2 Igneous rocks are **crystalline** solids that were formed from the cooling of magma. Magma is liquid rock that is found beneath the Earth's crust; we can see magma when a volcano erupts. When magma reaches the Earth's surface, it is called lava. When magma cools, it forms igneous rock. This category of rock makes up the majority of the rocks in the crust of the Earth. Geologists place igneous rocks into twelve subcategories based on their texture and composition. Texture refers to how large the individual mineral grains are in the rock. Composition refers to the minerals that are formed when the magma cools. Based on this **classification** system, some rocks are made of the exact same material but are considered different rocks because they have different textures.

crystalline   of or like crystal, clear, transparent

classification   the act of putting things into groups based on similar characteristics and traits

3 Although the majority of the Earth's crust is made of igneous rock, the Earth is covered with a thin layer of sedimentary rocks. When we look out at a landscape, it is mostly sedimentary rocks that we see. Sedimentary rocks are called secondary rocks because they are formed out of broken-off pieces of other rocks. This is called sediment. This sediment gets pressed together as more bits of rock press down on it. With enough pressure, the sediment becomes cemented together, forming a rock. Sedimentary rock forms in layers. As a result, when the side of a mountain has been cut open, we can sometimes see the layers of sedimentary rocks that have formed over thousands of years. There are three types of sedimentary rocks. Clastic is the most common type of sedimentary rock that is formed from bits of broken rocks. Chemical is formed when standing water evaporates, leaving behind **dissolved** minerals. This type of sedimentary rock is common in areas where seasonal lakes form. Organic is sedimentary rock that is formed by the accumulation of organic material. An example of this process can be found on seafloors. Many animals use **calcium** for shells, bones, and teeth. This calcium builds up on the seafloor forming organic sedimentary rock.

4 The final classification of rock is metamorphic rock. Metamorphic gets its name from meta (change) and morph (form). Any rock can become a metamorphic rock. All that is required is for the rock to be moved to conditions where the rock becomes **unstable**. The most common way in which this happens is for the rock to become buried, which leads to a rise in temperature and pressure. **Marble** is a common metamorphic rock.

5 The next time you look at a rock, see if you can tell what type of rock it is and how it was formed.

---

dissolve to break up, dismiss, disperse
calcium a white metallic element that makes up the bones of many animals and is needed by most living things

unstable inconsistent, changing
marble a hard, highly polished and smooth stone, usually cold to the touch

Vocabulary Study I

Match the word with its synonym.

1. majority   a. lava
2. grains   b. exterior
3. magma   c. bulk
4. formed   d. bits
5. surface   e. materialized

Reading comprehension I

Main idea

What's the passage about?

a. How different types of rocks are formed
b. What makes the Earth
c. Volcanoes
d. Sedimentary rocks

Detail questions

1. Cooled magma forms _____.
   a. sedimentary rock   b. igneous rock
   c. oceans   d. metamorphic rock

2. _____ is a common type of metamorphic rock.
   a. Sandstone   b. Diamond
   c. Marble   d. Granite

3. The three types of sedimentary rock are _____.
   a. clastic, chemical, and organic
   b. clastic, chemical, and magma
   c. magma, marble, and calcium
   d. igneous, sedimentary, and metamorphic

Vocabulary Study II

Word root: para

1. **parasol** = para (defense against) + sol (sun)
   parachute = para (defense against) + chute (fall)
   paranormal = para (beyond) + normal (usual)

2. **parasol:** defense against, sun → an umbrella used to block the sun
   parachute: defense against, fall → device used to slow a fall
   paranormal: beyond, usual → impossible to explain in a scientific way

3. Complete the following sentences choosing the right word.

parasol	parachute	paranormal

   a. Seeing a ghost is a _____ experience.

   b. If you plan to jump from a plan, you will need a _____ .

   c. She always carries a _____ on sunny days.

Reading comprehension II

Inference and purpose

The purpose of this passage is to inform the reader about _____ .

    a. types of rocks   b. how rocks are formed

    c. how different types of rocks are formed   d. how the Earth was formed

Coherence

Look at the four squares [■] that indicate where the following sentence can be added to the passage below. Where would the sentence best fit?

So metamorphic rocks are rocks that have gone through some sort of change.

■ The final classification of rock is metamorphic rock. ■ Metamorphic gets its name from meta (change) and morph (form). ■ Any rock can become a metamorphic rock. All that is required is for the rock to be moved to conditions where the rock becomes unstable. ■ The most common way in which this happens is for the rock to become buried, which leads to a rise in temperature and pressure. Marble is a common metamorphic rock.

Listening comprehension

Main idea

What is the lecture mainly about?

    a. The effects of earthquakes

    b. The role of pressure in everyday life

    c. The formation of sedimentary rocks

    d. The structure of the earth

Details

1. What is true about sediment?

    a. It is related to volcanoes.

    b. It is formed by earthquakes.

    c. It can form a rock in a certain situation.

    d. It is not associated with sedimentary rocks.

2. What is true about sedimentary rocks?

    a. There are five main types of them.

    b. They do not form layers.

    c. We can rarely see them.

    d. They are called secondary rocks.

Paraphrasing

A geologist can look at a rock and tell you its history and how and where it was formed.

Which of the sentences below best expresses the essential information in the highlighted sentence in the passage? Incorrect choices change the meaning in important ways or leave out essential information.

    a. Rocks can speak to geologists and tell their history.

    b. Geologists only look at rocks to tell their history and where they were formed.

    c. Geologists talk a lot about how and where rocks were formed

    d. All a geologist has to do is look at a rock to know the process that formed it and where it was formed.

Summary

Complete the following list by choosing the three true sentences about the passage.

-
-
-

a. Sedimentary rock is rock that has changed.

b. There are three classifications of rock.

c. Metamorphic rock is rock that is made of bits of other rocks.

d. Marble is a metamorphic rock.

e. Igneous rock is magma that has cooled.

f. Clastic rock is a type of metamorphic rock.

Speaking

What do you and your friends do for fun?

Model response

1. Fill in the blanks using the words in the box.

> weekends   money   shopping   money   window-shop   like

My friends and I like to go _____. Every chance we get, we go to the shopping mall. We don't have a lot of _____, but we still like to go and _____. This gives us a chance to see what the new styles are. If I see something I really _____, I will save my _____ until I can buy it. The shopping mall is also a great place to meet other people. A lot of people my age go there on the _____, so I can talk to and meet new people.

2. Using your own words, answer the question above. Then talk to the class.

19

Black Sunday

Pre-reading activity
1. What do you think of when you hear "dust bowl?"
2. Have you ever seen a dust storm?
3. What were the 1930s like in your country?

1 In the 1930s, the plains of America and **Canada** were hit with a series of devastating dust storms; the storms were so severe that this region became known as the "dust bowl." While most of the country was suffering through hard times due to the worldwide depression of 1929, the farm lands of the plains were enjoying some of the best years in history in 1930 and 1931. This productive and prosperous farmland would soon be hit by a combination of conditions that would devastate the region. Years of overfarming without crop rotation left the plains vulnerable to erosion. These poor farming practices coupled with a drought created conditions where the soil dried, making dust storms possible. When farmers plowed their fields, they left the dried soil exposed to the wind.

2 On November 11, 1933, the conditions of dry, exposed soil coupled with a strong wind produced the first in a series of severe dust storms. The once fertile topsoil blackened the sky, turning day as dark as night. The next year, conditions hadn't gotten any better. On May 11, 1934, a strong two-day dust storm hit the plains. The dust storms blew all the way to **Chicago**, hundreds of miles away. The storms dumped four pounds of dirt for every person in Chicago. Witnesses said that dirt fell like snow. Several days later, the storms

---

Canada   a country in North America located north of the United States

Chicago   a city in Illinois located in America's Midwest

New England   a group of states consisting of the northeast portion of the United States, including New York, Massachusetts, Vermont, Maine, etc.

reached the cities of the East Coast, a thousand miles away. The already suffering plains were hit by another year of drought and more storms. The worst of the dust storms struck on April 14, 1935; this became known as "Black Sunday." People reported not being able to see five feet in front of them during the day. During this period of dust storms, red snow fell on the cities of **New England**. After three years of drought, the once fertile plains were barren; farmers couldn't make a living, so many lost their farms.

3   To try to restore the land, newly elected President Franklin D. Roosevelt created the Soil Conservation Service, but it was too late for many. Families began to leave the plains in a mass migration. Estimates of one to two million people were displaced by the dust storms. Many of these people traveled to the Western states of California, **Oregon**, and Washington in search of work. They became known as Okies. These once profitable farmers had to move from town to town to find **temporary** work. Shantytowns sprang up on the outskirts of many towns. The Okies were often met with hostility and sometimes even violence as they competed for jobs with **locals**.

4   Today, the plains are once again fertile, profitable farm lands. There are still years of drought, but with proper land management the dust bowl days won't return.

Oregon   a state located in the northwest portion of the United States north of California and south of Washington

temporary   not permanent, lasting for a short time

local   a person from a particular area

Vocabulary Study I

Match the word with its synonym.

1. crop
2. prosperous
3. fertile
4. devastate
5. combination

a. mixture
b. destroy
c. farm product
d. bountiful
e. successful

Reading comprehension I

Main idea

What's the passage about?

a. The storms that destroyed farms in the plains
b. Farming
c. The migration of people to California, Oregon, and Washington
d. The depression during the 1930s

Detail questions

1. The worst of the dust storms was called _____.

   a. Muddy Monday
   b. Terrible Tuesday
   c. Black Sunday
   d. Windy Wednesday

2. People who left the dust bowl for the Western states were called

   _____.

   a. Okies
   b. Muddies
   c. Plainies
   d. Movers

3. The first in the series of dust storms was on _____.

   a. November 11, 1944
   b. November 11, 1833
   c. November 11, 1955
   d. November 11, 1933

Vocabulary Study II

Word root: dos, dot

1. **dose** = dose (to give)
   antidote = anti (against) + dot (to give)
   anecdote = an (not) + ec (out) + dot (to give)

2. **dose:** to give → an amount of medicine given
   antidote: against, to give → medicine given to counteract a poison
   anecdote: not, out, to give → a short story told

3. Complete the following sentences choosing the right word.

dose	antidote	anecdote

   a. The doctor gave the patient a _____ of medicine.

   b. The old man told an _____ about his early life.

   c. The man took an _____ for the snake bite.

Reading comprehension II

Inference and purpose

It can be inferred that a dust storm occurs when _____ .

   a. dry dirt is blown into the air   b. heavy rains wash the topsoil away

   c. snow freezes the topsoil   d. the topsoil becomes mud

Coherence

Look at the four squares [■] that indicate where the following sentence can be added to the passage below. Where would the sentence best fit?

> **By the time F. D. Roosevelt was elected President, many farmers had already lost their farms and had to look for other work.**

■ To try to restore the land, newly elected President Franklin D. Roosevelt created the Soil Conservation Service, but it was too late for many. ■ Families began to leave the plains in a mass migration. Estimates of one to two million people were displaced by the dust storms. Many of these people traveled to the Western states of California, Oregon, and Washington in search of work. ■ They became known as Okies. These once profitable farmers had to move from town to town to find temporary work. Shantytowns sprang up on the outskirts of many towns. ■ The Okies were often met with hostility and sometimes even violence as they competed for jobs with locals.

Listening comprehension

Main idea

What is the lecture mainly about?

a. The process of erosion

b. The cause of the dust bowl

c. Canadian plains

d. The Great Depression

Details

1. What is true about the dust bowl?

   a. It was beneficial to plains of America and Canada.

   b. It was a kind of hurricane.

   c. It refers to a series of dust storms.

   d. It was vulnerable to erosion.

2. What is true about the plains of America and Canada?

   a. They were not affected by erosion.

   b. All farmers left them in the 1930s.

   c. Their soil became dry in the 1930s.

   d. Crop rotation was popular in those areas in the 1930s.

Paraphrasing

> **To try to restore the land, newly elected President Franklin D. Roosevelt created the Soil Conservation Service, but it was too late for many.**

Which of the sentences below best expresses the essential information in the highlighted sentence in the passage? Incorrect choices change the meaning in important ways or leave out essential information.

a. The Soil Conservation Service created President Roosevelt in an effort to restore the land, but it was too late.

b. The Soil Conservation Service was created to restore the land.

c. President F. D. Roosevelt created the Soil Conservation Service.

d. Although it was too late for many, F. D. Roosevelt created the Soil Conservation Service in an effort to restore the land

Summary

Complete the following list by choosing the three true sentences about the passage.

-
-
-

a. The farms in the plains states were once very profitable.

b. The farms in the plains are profitable today.

c. Very few people left the plains during the dust storms of the 1930s

d. Most of the people who left the dust bowl went to Chicago.

e. The farms in the plains failed during the dust storms of the 1930s.

f. There are no farms in the plains today

Speaking

Why do people immigrate to other countries?

Model response

1. Fill in the blanks using the words in the box.

> countries   better   middle   stayed   language   immigrate

People immigrate to other _____ for many reasons. My family immigrated to the United States to escape famine. They lived in Ireland in the _____ part of the 1800s. Many people who _____ in Ireland died of starvation. Many people _____ to new countries to give their children a _____ life. I think it would be scary to move to a new country where I didn't even speak the _____ and people do things differently than I'm used to. To me, people who immigrate to other countries are brave.

2. Using your own words, answer the question above. Then talk to the class.

20

Louis Pasteur

Pre-reading activity
1. What causes disease?
2. What is a vaccination?
3. Have you heard of Louis Pasteur?

1 Louis Pasteur was born on December 27, 1822, in the Jura region of France. He earned a doctorate from the Ecole Normale in **Paris**, and after several years of teaching and conducting research, he was appointed professor of chemistry at the University of Lille. Part of the mission of the university was to find solutions to the practical problems faced by local industry, particularly in the production of alcoholic beverages. A major problem the industry had was that of spoilage. If the manufactures of alcoholic beverages could find a way to prevent their products from souring, the industry would be much more profitable.

2 Pasteur investigated the problem and was able to show that unseen organisms such as **bacteria** were responsible for the spoilage. He went further and found a solution to the problem. He discovered that the bacteria and other organisms could be removed by heating and then cooling the liquid. This process became known as Pasteurization. Pasteur was successful in solving the problem for the manufactures, but he wanted to find out where the bacteria came from.

3 The **prevailing** theory among scientists of the day said that bacteria were spontaneously generated within the substance. Pasteur undertook experiments that challenged this position. Through a series of experiments, he was able to show that bacteria were introduced from the environment. When he first

---

Paris the capital city of France, a country in Europe west of Germany and northeast of Spain

bacteria very small organisms that are made of a single cell and cannot be seen by the naked eye

presented his ideas, they were rejected by most of his peers, but by 1864 the French Academy of Sciences accepted Pasteur's conclusions. His studies convinced them that the theory of germ contamination as the cause of disease was correct.

4 The germ contamination theory states that germs attack the body from outside and cause disease. Many people of the time didn't believe that such small organisms could be the cause of disease and death in larger organisms. Pasteur began to work on cholera in chickens. During his work, a culture of the cholera germs had spoiled and failed to produce the disease in chickens when exposed to the spoiled **batch**. Later, Pasteur tried to infect these chickens with a fresh batch of the cholera germ, but found that they remained healthy. The weakened spoiled batch of cholera had made them immune to subsequent infection. In the 1870s, he used this immunization method to protect cattle against **anthrax**. The idea of immunization was not new, as Edward Jenner had successfully vaccinated people against smallpox using cowpox as early as 1796. The difference was that the weakened form of the diseases was being made artificially, and a naturally weakened form of the disease did not have to be found. This revolutionized the treatment of infectious diseases. Pasteur gave the weakened form of these diseases the name of vaccines.

5 Pasteur died in 1895 after a series of **strokes**. He was a national hero and received a state funeral. In a recent listing of the one hundred most influential people in history, Pasteur was listed at number eleven.

---

prevailing dominant
batch a quantity of materials prepared or required for one operation

anthrax an infectious, often, fatal disease of cattle, sheep, or other mammals
stroke a blockage of a blood vessel to the brain which can lead to paralysis or even death

Vocabulary Study I

Match the word with its synonym.

1. practical
2. spoil
3. investigate
4. major
5. process

a. analyze
b. ruin
c. pragmatic
d. procedure
e. foremost

Reading comprehension I

Main idea

What's the passage about?

a. Bacteria
b. Germs
c. Chemistry
d. Louis Pasteur

Detail questions

1. A major problem that the alcoholic beverages manufacturers had was

   _____.

   a. spoilage
   b. people didn't like the taste
   c. the expense of production
   d. difficulty finding ingredients

2. In Pasteur's time, most scientists thought that bacteria came from _____.
   a. cats
   b. outside the substance
   c. dogs
   d. within the substance

3. The first person to use immunization to fight disease was _____.
   a. Jenner
   b. Pasteur
   c. Edison
   d. Einstein

Vocabulary Study II

Word root: spec(t)

1. **prospect** = pro (forward) + spect (look)
   inspect = in (into) + spect (look)
   expect = ex (out) + spect (look)

2. **prospect:** forward, look → to look at the future, possibility
   inspect: into, look → look at closely
   expect: out, look → anticipate

3. Complete the following sentences choosing the right word.

prospect	inspect	expected

   a. He studied hard and _____ to get a good grade.

   b. The _____ of seeing her again is pleasant.

   c. The teacher will _____ the examination papers to be sure no one cheated.

Reading comprehension II

Inference and purpose

It can be inferred from the passage that _____ .

   a. Pasteur died penniless   b. Pasteur believed in astrology

   c. Pasteur was admired by many people   d. Pasteur won the Nobel Prize

Coherence

Look at the four squares [■] that indicate where the following sentence can be added to the passage below. Where would the sentence best fit?

Today, this same method is used to prevent spoilage in many products, saving companies billions of dollars every year.

■ Pasteur investigated the problem and was able to show that unseen organisms such as bacteria were responsible for the spoilage. ■ He went further and found a solution to the problem. He discovered that the bacteria and other organisms could be removed by heating and then cooling the liquid. This process became known as Pasteurization. ■ Pasteur was successful in solving the problem for the manufactures, but he wanted to find out where the bacteria came from. ■

Listening comprehension

Main idea

What is the lecture mainly about?

a. The French Academy of Sciences

b. Contamination of drinking water

c. Pasteur's discovery concerning bacteria

d. The significance of the environment

Details

1. What is true about Pasteur?

    a. Most of his peers accepted his new discovery.

    b. He was against conducting scientific experiments.

    c. He regarded germ contamination as the cause of disease.

    d. He won the Nobel Prize in 1864.

2. What is true about the French Academy of Sciences?

    a. It expelled Pasteur.

    b. It was rejected by most scientists.

    c. It was established in London.

    d. It supported Pasteur's ideas.

Paraphrasing

The prevailing theory among scientists of the day said that bacteria were spontaneously generated within the substance.

Which of the sentences below best expresses the essential information in the highlighted sentence in the passage? Incorrect choices change the meaning in important ways or leave out essential information.

a. No one believed that bacteria were spontaneously generated within substances during Pasteur's life.

b. The only theory during Pasteur's time was that bacteria were spontaneously generated within substances.

c. At the time most scientists believed that bacteria were spontaneously generated within substance.

d. Scientists in Pasteur's time knew that bacteria were spontaneously generated within substances.

Summary

Complete the following list by choosing the three true sentences about the passage.

-
-
-

    a. Pasteur showed that unseen organisms such as bacteria caused spoilage.

    b. Bacteria come from within substances.

    c. Pasteur's theories were unproven when he died.

    d. Pasteur made advancements in the use of immunizations.

    e. Pasteur was the first person to use immunization to fight disease.

    f. Jenner used cowpox to inoculate people against smallpox.

Speaking

Is there a question that you always wanted to know the answer to?

Model response

1. Fill in the blanks using the words in the box.

> reflection   know   people   reason   sky   sunlight

I have always wanted to _____ why the sky is blue. _____ have told me different answers, but I don't know what the real _____ is. My mother told me that the sky is blue because of the _____ of the oceans, but my best friend told me that the _____ is blue because the _____ is bent as it enters the atmosphere, like a rainbow. I don't know which answer is right or if the real reason is something else.

2. Using your own words, answer the question above. Then talk to the class.

Develop and Refine Your Reading Strategies
in Preparation for the New TOEFL iBT Tests

New Strategic
Reading Level 3

W **WorldCom ELT**

New Strategic Reading

Level 3

Vocabulary & Idioms

throne	*n.*	the seat of a king, bishop, queen, etc.
		Ex. The king sat with two guards on either side of his throne.
realm	*n.*	kingdom
		Ex. The Queen's realm stretched from Scotland to Italy.
fascination	*n.*	the state of being intensely interested or attracted
		Ex. I have a fascination with books.
philosopher	*n.*	a person who offers views on ethics, logic, etc.
		Ex. Aristotle was a great philosopher.
mimic	*v.*	to copy, to imitate
		Ex. Please stop mimicking the way I speak.
progress	*n.*	improvement, advancement
		Ex. We've made much progress with computer technology in recent years.
forerunner	*n.*	one that precedes in time, a predecessor
		Ex. The typewriter is a forerunner of the printer.
doomed	*adj.*	determined by a tragic fate
		Ex. He was doomed to misery for his misdeeds.
conceive	*v.*	to come up with, to think of
		Ex. She conceived of the idea of putting strawberries inside the drink.
parachute	*n.*	a umbrella-like device used to allow a person to float down safely from a great height such as from a plane
		Ex. He jumped out of the plane and quickly opened his parachute.
commonplace	*adj.*	ordinary, normal, common
		Ex. Eating fast food is now commonplace for busy workers of the city.
prototype	*n.*	the original or model on which something is based
		Ex. Please show us the prototype for the new product.

Speaking Task #1

▶ Do you join a cyber-community? What is it and why is it important to you?

Model Response

1. Fill in the blanks using the words in the box:

> called   chances   many   sense   show   true   trying   unlike   who

I belong to a cyber-community _____ *Pen Pals United*. This
community is important to me in _____ ways. First, my cyber-
community gives me _____ to write a letter by hand. I think this is
very important because we are _____ to keep the tradition of
writing letters by hand. _____ an email, a letter written by hand can
_____ your true feelings to other people. Second, I meet a lot of
people _____ firmly believe that _____ friendship is
important in this busy world. In this _____, my cyber-community is
just like a family.

2. Using your own words, answer the question above. Then talk to the class.

Speak Clearly

3. Complete the sentences choosing the right answer from the box below:

> • to keep the tradition of writing a letter by hand
> • should write a letter by hand
> • convenient than sending a hand-written letter

(a) Some people still believe that we _____.

(b) Sending an e-mail is more _____.

(c) Some people are trying hard _____.

Vocabulary & Idioms

superstar	*n.*	a person who is esteemed for his exceptional talent as an actor, singer, etc.
		Ex. Michael Jordan was a basketball superstar.
compose	*v.*	to write music
		Ex. Mozart composed countless pieces that are still played today.
gifted	*adj.*	talented
		Ex. He is gifted at painting.
blindfolded	*adj.*	unable to see because of something wrapped around the eyes
		Ex. Some children can play the piano blindfolded.
fancy	*adj.*	expensive
		Ex. He always throws very fancy parties.
lavish	*adj.*	describing one who uses or gives too much
		Ex. Because of his lavish lifestyle, he spent of the money that he earned.
work ethic		belief in the importance of hard work
		Ex. You must improve your work ethic if you wish to attend medical school.
debt	*n.*	something that is owed
		Ex. It is very dangerous to fall into debt.
commission	*n.*	payment
		Ex. He paid commission to the artist.
score	*n.*	a written piece of music with all the instrumental and vocal parts included
		Ex. The movie score was very emotional.
testament	*n.*	proof
		Ex. Please provide testament of your talents.
fragile	*adj.*	easily broken, damaged, frail
		Ex. The contents of the box are very fragile.

Writing Task #1

▸ Why do you think we should respect the poor?

Model Response

1. Fill in the blanks using the words in the box:

> | in | like | may | neat | of | sense | should | smile |
> | therefore | accidents | become | care | else | feelings |

_____ my opinion, we ought to respect poor people for three main reasons.

First _____ all, it is the right thing to do. These days, people do not _____ about the right things we should do. But if something is the right thing to do, we _____ do it. That is our common _____.

Second, the poor are human beings just _____ us. They also have their own thoughts and _____. When they are happy, they _____. When they are sad, they cry. Maybe they do not wear _____ clothes, but that does not matter. What matters is that they should be respected just like everybody _____.

Finally, anybody can _____ poor. You see, _____ happen and they can make you poor. You _____ lose your job and become poor. In this sense, the poor are just ordinary people who have bad luck. _____, they should be treated just like ordinary people.

2. Using your own words, answer the question above. Write your answer on a separate sheet of paper.

Write Clearly

3. Complete the sentences choosing the right answer from the box below:

> • respect all people
> • will happen to them

(a) We should _____.

(b) Nobody knows what _____.

Vocabulary & Idioms

ecosystem	*n.*	a community of organisms and its environment
		Ex. The ecosystem contains many different types of plants and animals.
interior	*n.*	inside
		Ex. The interior of the house was quite spacious.
stadium	*n.*	a sports arena, usually oval in shape with many tiers of seats and spectators
		Ex. The football players stormed into the stadium.
observatory	*n.*	a building used for watching the stars and the planets
		Ex. You can see Saturn if you go to the observatory.
threaten	*v.*	to present a danger to
		Ex. The storm clouds threatened the farmer's fields.
billboard	*n.*	a large flat board where advertisements are placed
		Ex. There was a large ad for cigarettes on the billboard.
incidence	*n.*	occurrence
		Ex. The incidence was not normal.
disrupt	*v.*	to cause turmoil or disorder, to interrupt
		Ex. The loud chirping disrupted my sleep.
navigation	*n.*	the act of finding one's way
		Ex. Navigation is difficult in this area because of the fog.
nocturnal	*adj.*	active at night
		Ex. Owls and mice are example of nocturnal animals.
salamander	*n.*	a small lizard-like animal
		Ex. As young children, we used to catch salamanders in the creek.
reproduce	*v.*	to produce one or more individuals through sexual or asexual activity
		Ex. Spring is a prime time for animals to reproduce.

Speaking Task #2

▸ Some students exercise outdoors to get fit. Others prefer to meditate.
Which do you think is better for students and why?

Model Response

1. Fill in the blanks using the words in the box:

> calm   enables   go   hand   health   in   lead   safer   when

_____ my opinion, meditating is better for students than exercising

outdoors. First of all, meditating is a _____ way of getting fit. People

often get hurt _____ they try to work out too hard. On the other

_____, you cannot meditate too hard. Second, meditating helps you

let _____ of stress and remain _____, which is very good

for physical and mental _____. This _____ to strength and

fitness. In short, meditating _____ students to get fit without a risk.

2. Using your own words, answer the question above. Then talk to the class.

Speak Clearly

3. Complete the sentences choosing the right answer from the box below:

> • too hard
> • become truly healthy
> • much better

(a) When we let go of stress, we can _____.

(b) By exercising outdoors, we can feel _____.

(c) Don't try to do anything _____.

Vocabulary & Idioms

unimpressive   *adj.* not having the ability of producing a strong vivid effect
Ex. Your baseball record is unimpressive.

frail   *adj.* weak
Ex. His frail body was no match in a fight against his brother's bulky arms.

passionate   *adj.* having strong desire and emotion
Ex. He is very passionate about science.

privileged   *adj.* belonging to a class that enjoys special rights or privileges
Ex. You're very privileged to be able to walk around with so many bodyguards.

upbringing   *n.* the rearing and training during childhood
Ex. He had a poor upbringing.

orthodox   *adj.* adhering to traditionally accepted principles, especially of a religion
Ex. The church does not follow orthodox practices.

mediocre   *adj.* of only ordinary or moderate quality
Ex. The restaurant's food is very mediocre.

vow   *n.* promise
Ex. I made a vow to quit smoking.

frequent   *v.* to visit often
Ex. I frequent the museum.

venture   *n.* a business enterprise
Ex. His cafe venture failed and he lost a large sum of money.

fateful   *adj.* decisively important
Ex. It was a fateful day when he became ill.

homogenous   *adj.* all of the same or similar kind in nature
Ex. Japanese society is very homogenous because of the lack of foreigners.

Writing Task #2

▶ What do you think tsunamis teach us?

Model Response

1. Fill in the blanks using the words in the box:

alone	connected	different	every	getting	mainly
much	part	sense	should	strong	such	together

In my opinion, we can learn three _____ things from tsunamis.

First of all, they remind us that we are closely _____ with nature. We often forget this simple fact: We are _____ of nature. I think this is _____ because technology gives us a false message about our relationship with nature. _____ time we hurt nature, we hurt ourselves.

Second, tsunamis teach us that we _____ be humble. Technology is _____ better and better, but we cannot control or conquer nature. In many ways, we are children of Mother Nature, and just like our mothers nature is _____ stronger than we are.

Finally, tsunamis show us that we can become _____ when we work together. When we are _____, we are weak. But when we are _____, we can do great things. Together, we can even overcome great disasters _____ as tsunamis. In this _____, tsunamis show us who we really are.

2. Using your own words, answer the question above. Write your answer on a separate sheet of paper.

Write Clearly

3. Complete the sentences choosing the right answer from the box below:

- respect Mother Nature
- or kill a lot of people

(a) Tsunamis can hurt _____.

(b) We should _____.

📖 Vocabulary & Idioms

plank	*n.*	a long flat piece of wood
		Ex. Let's use these planks to build a small shed.
admire	*v.*	to look at with pleasure, wonder, or approval
		Ex. I really admire his artwork.
missionary	*n.*	one who is sent on a mission, especially to do religious or charitable work in a foreign country
		Ex. The Christian missionaries worked hard to convert the natives.
comeback	*n.*	a return
		Ex. After disappearing for a few years, the singer made a comeback.
overthrow	*n.*	the act of putting an end to a government by force
		Ex. The rebellion strived for the overthrow of the king and queen.
shore	*n.*	the land along the edge of a sea, lake, etc.
		Ex. It will take a few minutes to swim back to the shore.
medal	*n.*	a piece of medal given as an award for a competition, contest, tournament, etc.
		Ex. He received a medal for first place.
capsize	*v.*	to turn up, to overturn
		Ex. A large wave caused the raft to capsize.
lifeguard	*n.*	an expert swimmer whose job is to protect and rescue swimmers from drowning
		Ex. It could be dangerous here since there are no lifeguards.
avid	*adj.*	enthusiastic
		Ex. He is an avid believer of Jesus Christ.
devotee	*n.*	one who gives time, attention, or self to an activity
		Ex. The animals' rights devotees marched in front of the White House.
budget	*n.*	the total money available for a purpose
		Ex. Our shopping budget is under twenty dollars.

Speaking Task #3

▶ If you could change one thing about your body, what would it be? Tell us why.

Model Response

1. Fill in the blanks using the words in the box:

> anyway besides choice lie mainly own power until without worse

If I could have the _____ to change one thing about my body, I would change my eyes. This is _____ because I do not want to wear glasses anymore. My eyesight was normal _____ I was 15, but after that it got _____. So I had no _____ but to wear glasses. I have always wanted to see the world again with my _____ eyes, _____ the help of glasses. _____, our ability to see has always fascinated me. Do you know that our eyes cannot tell a _____? _____, I would like to have good eyesight again.

2. Using your own words, answer the question above. Then talk to the class.

Speak Clearly

3. Complete the sentences choosing the right answer from the box below:

> • not to use biotechnology for wrong purposes
> • many people's lives
> • do lots of wonderful things

(a) Biotechnology will change _____.

(b) With the help of biotechnology, we could _____.

(c) We should be careful _____.

 ## Vocabulary & Idioms

exotic   *adj.* foreign, unusual
Ex. *This dish has a very exotic taste.*

slaughter   *v.* the killing of a great number of people or animals
Ex. *The farmer prepared to slaughter the cows.*

verge   *n.* the limit or point beyond which something will happen, brink
Ex. *The operation was on the verge of disaster.*

conservationist   *n.* one who supports the preservation of the environment and natural resources
Ex. *Conservationists have worked hard to fund the national park.*

habitat   *n.* the natural environment for a living thing
Ex. *The desert provides a natural habitat for the cactus.*

inspiration   *n.* arousal of the mind to special activity or creativity
Ex. *The writer searched for inspiration for his new novel.*

plantation   *n.* a very large farm or estate in tropical or semitropical climates where tobacco, cotton, sugar cane, coffee, etc. is grown, usually by resident laborers
Ex. *The plantation owner had many slaves working in his fields.*

stepmother   *n.* the wife of one's father by a later marriage
Ex. *My father married my stepmother a few years after he divorced my mother.*

conscription   *n.* required or obligatory enrollment into the military
Ex. *The government issued a conscription of men in preparation for war.*

estate   *n.* a large piece of property with an elaborate house
Ex. *His estate stretched for miles.*

band   *v.* to mark, decorate, or furnish with a thin flat strip of material or band
Ex. *He banded his fingers with strips of green for St. Patrick's Day.*

prospect   *n.* outlook for the future
Ex. *Business prospects were low.*

Writing Task #3

▶ Do you believe that new technology like MP3 technology makes people happy?

Model Response

1. Fill in the blanks using the words in the box:

connected	course	lead	mainly	means	nothing
opinion	purpose	short	unhappy	used	

   In my _____, new technology does not _____ to our happiness.

   First of all, the _____ of technology is not to make people happy, but to make people's lives more convenient. Some people may think that convenience _____ happiness. But it does not. When we feel that we are _____ with our surrounding world, we can feel true happiness. Convenience has _____ to do with that feeling.

   Second, new technology can make us _____. This is _____ because there are a lot of ways to use technology for bad purposes. For example, nuclear technology can be _____ to make nuclear weapons, which can kill lots of people. Of _____, we can use the same technology for good purposes, but that does not mean it will make us happy.

   In _____, new technology itself does not make us happy.

2. Using your own words, answer the question above. Write your answer on a separate sheet of paper.

Write Clearly

3. Complete the sentences choosing the right answer from the box below:

   - do bad things
   - to do good things
   - the same as happiness

   (a) Convenience is not _____.

   (b) Technology can be used to _____.

   (c) We should use technology _____.

Vocabulary & Idioms

feeding ground
n. area where an animal goes to eat
Ex. The birds flocked to the new feeding ground.

current
n. a large body of water or air moving in a certain direction
Ex. The current carried the raft down the river.

peninsula
n. an area of land surrounded on three sides by water
Ex. Florida and Korea are examples of peninsulas.

boundary
n. something that indicates bounds or limits, border
Ex. The countries experience many conflicts near their shared boundary.

nickname
n. a name given as a substitute for the actual or proper name
Ex. Because he was so smart, his friends gave him the nickname "Brains."

indigo
adj. having a deep violet to grayish blue color
Ex. The garden was filled with indigo flowers.

highway
n. a main, ordinary track or route
Ex. The travelers followed the usual highway that had been marked previously.

destination
n. the place to which a person travels
Ex. Our final destination is New York City.

complaint
n. a expression of discontent, grief, lamentation, etc.
Ex. There were many complaints about the service at the restaurant.

progress
n. forward or onward movement
Ex. Progress was slow at the factories today.

ignorant
adj. lacking in knowledge or training
Ex. He was ignorant of the required work knowledge for his job due to lack of training.

oceanographer
n. one who studies the physical geography of the ocean
Ex. The oceanographer researched the area of the Atlanta Ocean in hopes of finding new phenomena.

Speaking Task #4

▶ Some children like playing violent computer games. Others play non-violent games. Which do you think is better for children and why?

Model Response

1. Fill in the blanks using the words in the box:

> coming different dull experience feel opinion other to under unlike

In my _____, playing non-violent computer games is much, much better for children. First of all, such games really help children to let go of stress _____ from their everyday lives. _____ what many people believe, today's children are _____ a lot of stress, and one way of letting go of such stress is to do something quite _____ from daily activities. Playing non-violent games gives such _____ in a harmless way. On the _____ hand, violent games give us a lot of stress because the experience of losing a game makes us _____ really bad. Such games also make us emotionally _____. Therefore, playing non-violent games is a better way _____ let go of stress.

2. Using your own words, answer the question above. Then talk to the class.

Speak Clearly

3. Complete the sentences choosing the right answer from the box below:

> • let go of stress
> • an extremely busy life
> • are bad for children

(a) Many people believe that violent computer games _____.

(b) In order to get fit, we need to _____.

(c) Today's children live _____.

Vocabulary & Idioms

pastime   *n.*   recreation, something that serves to pass time agreeably
            Ex. Reading is a favorite pastime of mine.

league   *n.*   a group of athletic teams that compete amongst themselves
            Ex. The football league championship game is next week.

export   *n.*   something that is transmitted or sent to another country
            Ex. Fireworks is an export of Ancient China.

hall of fame   a room or building set aside to honor outstanding individuals in any profession, locality, nation, etc.
            Ex. He was honored in the hall of fame for his record of achievements.

panel   *n.*   a group of people gathered to conduct a public discussion, judge a contest, serve as advisors, etc.
            Ex. The panel gathered to review the company's monthly earnings.

endorse   *v.*   to approve, support, or sustain
            Ex. Congress endorsed the new law.

questionable   *adj.*   doubtful or uncertain
            Ex. The evidence is questionable.

debate   *n.*   a discussion involving opposing viewpoints
            Ex. My mother and I had a debate about how much food we should buy for the party.

stool   *n.*   a single seat on legs without a back or arms
            Ex. The men sat on the stools drinking beer.

widely   *adv.* by a large number of people
            Ex. He is a widely known movie director.

mobile   *adj.*   capable of moving
            Ex. The Venus's-flytrap is an example of a mobile plant.

induct   *v.*   to admit as a member, to receive
            Ex. The president inducted him into the company.

Writing Task #4

▶ Tell us about your drawing experience.

Model Response

1. Fill in the blanks using the words in the box:

> activity   change   describe   enjoy   kinds   like   mainly
> maybe quite   same   sense   showed   special

   In my school days, I did not _____ drawing pictures. This was _____ because I was not good at drawing. So art teachers did not like my pictures. I guess my pictures did not _____ people or things in a natural way. In my pictures people became some _____ of monsters. They were either too tall or too short. The _____ was true for things. They were either too large or too small.

   Maybe I did not have any _____ of balance. I think this could explain my world in those days. It was full of _____ and insecurity. I did not feel safe or secure. I worried about too many things _____ my grades and my relationships with friends. _____ my pictures in those days were a reflection of my inner world.

   But I felt something _____ about drawing. The _____ made me see the world in many different ways. Sometimes I could feel very special because my pictures were _____ different from those of my friends. In a sense, drawing pictures _____ me that I was quite different from other people.

   In short, my drawing experience was a special one.

2. Using your own words, answer the question above. Write your answer on a separate sheet of paper.

Write Clearly

3. Complete the sentences choosing the right answer from the box below:

> • be a lot of fun   • in many different ways

   (a) Drawing pictures can _____.
   (b) We can see the world _____.

The California Gold Rush

 ## Vocabulary & Idioms

thriving	*adj.*	prospering, fortunate, successful
		Ex. His business was thriving.
mill	*n.*	a factory that manufactures certain kinds of goods such as paper or textiles
		Ex. Philadelphia is famous for its many steel mills.
suspicion	*n.*	the act of believing something is the case or is likely or possible
		Ex. My suspicion is that he is the culprit.
shrewd	*adj.*	very smart, tricky
		Ex. The shrewd man was always coming up with new ideas for his business.
teem	*v.*	to be full of things
		Ex. The water was teeming with tiny fish.
prospector	*n.*	one who searches an area for mineral deposits or oil
		Ex. Prospectors arrived in search of silver.
boomtown	*n.*	a town experiencing a sudden growth in economy or population
		Ex. The city was a boomtown in the late 19th century.
influx	*n.*	an inflow
		Ex. There was an influx of immigrants after the war.
shanty	*n.*	a crudely built cabin, hut, or house
		Ex. The man only had enough money to stay in a shanty for the time being.
abandon	*v.*	to give up, leave
		Ex. I abandoned my car after I ran out of fuel.
anchor	*v.*	to drop heavy chained device or anchor in the water in order to keep a ship fixed firmly
		Ex. We anchored the ship next to the port.
vial	*n.*	a small container for liquids
		Ex. The vial contained a pink liquid.

Speaking #5

▶ What is your favorite poem? Tell us why.

Model Response

1. Fill in the blanks using the words in the box:

> bright   famous   lived   misses   that   whenever   who   wrote

Do you know _____ Li Po is? He is a _____ Chinese poet.
Once he _____ a poem entitled "On a Quiet Night" and
_____ is my favorite poem. In this poem, he says that he
_____ his hometown so much. When he looks up at the
_____ moon, he thinks about his faraway hometown. I like this
poem a lot because I have _____ so many years away from my
hometown. I also miss my hometown so much, and _____ the bright
moon rises, I recite this poem.

2. Using your own words, answer the question above. Then talk to the class.

Speak Clearly

3. Complete the sentences choosing the right answer from the box below:

> • you will miss your family
> • it pours
> • they can express human feelings so beautifully

(a) A lot of people love poems because _____ .

(b) When you live away from your home, _____ .

(c) Whenever it rains, _____ .

unit 10 Auroras

 ## Vocabulary & Idioms

dawn   *n.*   morning during the sunrise
Ex. The rooster crowed at dawn.

mythology   *n.*   a body of myths
Ex. There are numerous gods in Greek mythology.

herring   *n.*   a type of food fish
Ex. The fisherman's catch consisted mostly of herring.

flash   *n.*   a sudden burst of light
Ex. Lightning flashes could be seen in the distance

school   *n.*   a large number of fish feeding or migrating together
Ex. The school of tuna swam swiftly away from danger.

polar   *adj.*   relating to the North Pole and South Pole
Ex. The weather was so cold that it resembled polar conditions.

solar   *adj.*   relating to the sun
Ex. Scientists are still researching new ways to make solar powered cars.

disrupt   *v.*   to cause disorder or turmoil
Ex. The kids playing outside my door disrupted my focus on my homework.

malfunction   *v.*   to fail to function properly
Ex. The computer is malfunctioning.

transmission   *n.*   communication
Ex. The airplane received a transmission from the control tower.

brilliant   *adj.*   bright
Ex. The brilliant light shone.

telegraph   *n.*   a communications system that allows the transmission of messages or signals to a distant place
Ex. Telegraphs were popular before the invention of the telephone.

Writing Task #5

▸ What is your favorite short story? Tell us about it.

Model Response

1. Fill in the blanks using the words in the box:

> bought   can't   combs   each   ever   greatest   had
> just   for   most   poor   reminds   written

   My favorite short story is "The Gift of the Magi" _____ by O Henry. In this short story, O Henry tells us about Della and Jim. They were a _____ couple. It was Christmas Eve. But they did not have enough money to buy a present for _____ other.

   So Della sold her long hair and _____ a platinum chain for Jim's gold watch. When Jim came home, she told him she _____ sold her hair. Jim was very surprised. This was because he sold his gold watch and bought beautiful _____ for Della's long hair.

   O Henry tells us that Della and Jim were the wisest of all the people who had _____ given presents. I agree with him. Of course, Della and Jim were _____ a poor couple. But I believe that they knew what is the _____ important thing in the world. In my opinion, that is selfless love _____ other people.

   In fact, when others are not happy, we _____ be happy. And when we truly love others, all of us can feel the _____ happiness. In this sense, Della and Jim were the happiest of all. So I love this short story which always _____ us of the importance of love.

2. Using your own words, answer the question above. Write your answer on a separate sheet of paper.

Write Clearly

3. Complete the sentences choosing the right answer from the box below:

> • be the happiest of all   • short story writers

   (a) O Henry was one of the greatest _____.
   (b) Poor people can _____.

Vocabulary & Idioms

bullring	*n.*	an arena for a bullfight
		Ex. The bullring erupted with cheers from the audience.
origin	*n.*	the point at which something comes into existence
		Ex. The origins of the custom is unknown.
custom	*n.*	a practice followed by a particular group or region
		Ex. Using chopsticks to eat is an Asian custom.
corral	*n.*	an enclosure or pen for horses, cattle, etc.
		Ex. Choose a horse from the corral.
youngster	*n.*	a child, young person
		Ex. The youngster had yet to learn proper manners and behavior.
gore	*v.*	to piece with a horn or tusk
		Ex. The elephant gored the other elephant with its large tusk.
barricade	*n.*	a barrier that is hastily constructed to defend
		Ex. We set up barricades around the house to keep out wild animals.
alert	*v.*	to warn
		Ex. The forecast alerted that a storm was approaching.
overtake	*v.*	to catch up with and pass
		Ex. The racecar eventually overtook the other and won the race.
herd	*n.*	a number of animals kept, feeding, or traveling together
		Ex. The herd of cattle fed off the grass in the field.
stray	*adj.*	found occurring apart from the others
		Ex. There were a few stray hairs on his cheek where he had missed shaving.
taunt	*v.*	to tease
		Ex. The children taunted the new teacher.

Speaking Task #6

▶ Some students are very proud of their country. Others do not care about their country. Which do you think is better for students and why?

Model Response

1. Fill in the blanks using the words in the box:

> badly   being   cases   every   overcome   particular   prove   realize   survive

In my opinion, _____ proud of their country is better for students for two main reasons. First of all, even in this highly globalized world, we cannot _____ and prosper without our country. There are too many examples that _____ this point. In _____, those people who do not have their own country are treated _____ in many cases. So, if you have your own country, then you have _____ reason to be proud of the country. Second, being proud of their country will help students try very hard to _____ their dreams. In such _____, doing their best is the same as loving their country, which will give them power to _____ many difficulties.

2. Using your own words, answer the question above. Then talk to the class.

Speak Clearly

3. Complete the sentences choosing the right answer from the box below:

> • to keep the tradition of writing a letter by hand
> • should write a letter by hand
> • convenient than sending a hand-written letter

(a) Most of us are _____.

(b) It is your duty to _____.

(c) Our love for our country will make us _____.

Vocabulary & Idioms

background	*n.*	one's origin, education, experience, etc. in relation to one's present character, status, etc.
		Ex. He came from a very wealthy background.
border	*n.*	boundary, edge
		Ex. The western border of the United States touches the Pacific Ocean.
scale	*v.*	to climb
		Ex. We scaled the mountain in three days.
summit	*n.*	the top of a mountain, the highest point
		Ex. The summit of the mountain reached through the clouds.
conquer	*v.*	to master, overcome
		Ex. They finally conquered the video game.
expedition	*n.*	a group of persons, ships, etc. on an excursion, journey, etc.
		Ex. He was the leader of the expedition.
sweets	*n.*	pie, cake, candy, etc.
		Ex. The kids held out their hands for sweets.
celebrity	*n.*	a famous or well-known person
		Ex. Fans rushed in to meet the celebrity.
peak	*n.*	a mountain with a pointed summit
		Ex. The peak is always covered in snow.
director	*n.*	a manager of a school
		Ex. The director of the school rejected the proposal.
mountaineering	*n.*	the sport of climbing mountains
		Ex. Mountaineering is a difficult and dangerous sport.
institute	*n.*	a school that is usually beyond the secondary school level that teaches technical subjects, usually separate but sometimes part of a university
		Ex. The institute of technology is famous for its quality education.

Writing Task #6

▸ Do you have a long-lost friend? Tell us about him or her.

Model Response

1. Fill in the blanks using the words in the box:

> ages   anyway   attend   behavior   care   completely
> couldn't   grade   however   parted   realize   same
> strange   than   together   while   who

I have a friend _____ I miss so much. I haven't seen him for _____. His name is Oz Shin, and he is really special. When I first met him, we were in the fifth _____. I was a country boy, _____ he was a city boy. I was surprised by everything he did. His speech and _____ were quite different from mine. And in a sense I admired him.

As time went by, _____, I learned how to do almost everything he could do. Then, we entered middle school _____. I got better grades on the exams _____ he did. But he started to say things that I _____ understand. He asked me questions like these: "What do our lives mean?" "Why can we not be people?" "What is happiness?" I just didn't understand why he asked me those _____ questions.

I just focused on my study and did not _____ about him. After a while, Oz got sick and did not _____ classes for some time. When he came to school again, all my friends were surprised at his face. He looked _____ different. Then we _____ from each other.

When I look back on those days, I _____ how important he was to me. In a sense, he was a good teacher. Today, I often ask myself the _____ question that Oz asked me. *What is happiness?* Nobody knows. _____, I miss him so much and want to see him again.

2. Using your own words, answer the question above. Write your answer on a separate sheet of paper.

📖 Vocabulary & Idioms

slavery　　*n.*　the state of being bound to servitude as property of a slave owner or household
Ex. Slavery was persistent in early American history.

drive　　*v.*　to cause and guide the movement of
Ex. The farmer drove the cattle back into the barn.

haul　　*v.*　to cart or transport
Ex. He hauled the materials back to the house.

innate　　*adj.*　existing in one since birth
Ex. Her innate abilities made her a fast learner in dance class.

sustain　　*v.*　to suffer
Ex. She sustained a blow to the head.

overseer　　*n.*　supervisor, manager
Ex. The overseer made sure the laborers continued to work.

scar　　*n.*　a mark left by a healed wound
Ex. I have a scar from when I burned myself.

seizure　　*n.*　a sudden attack, spasm, or convulsion, as in epilepsy or another disorder
Ex. The violent shaking indicated a seizure.

aged　　*adj.*　old
Ex. I was able to buy aged furniture for a cheap price.

scout　　*n.*　a soldier sent out to gather information
Ex. The army sent several scouts into enemy territory to gather information.

memorial　　*n.*　something built in order to remember a person or an event
Ex. The workers erected a war memorial.

bestow　　*v.*　to present as a gift or honor
Ex. He was bestowed with a medal for his bravery.

Speaking Task #7

▸ Do you have any dream that you remember vividly? What is it and why?

Model Response

1. Fill in the blanks using the words in the box:

> about   burning   dream   enter   grades   nervous   shows   sudden   there

I dream the same _____ again and again. In this dream, I am _____ to take a very important exam. I have studied for many days, _____ the candle at both ends. I _____ the classroom where I take the exam. But there is no one there. The time comes, but nobody _____ up. I wait and wait, sweating. Still, _____ is only me in the classroom. Then, all of a _____, the walls fall down, and I scream. I think I have this dream because I am very _____ about exams. I always worry about my _____ on the exams.

2. Using your own words, answer the question above. Write your answer on a separate sheet of paper.

Speak Clearly

3. Complete the sentences choosing the right answer from the box below:

> • are very frightening
> • about anything

(a) Dreams can be _____.
(b) Some dreams _____.

Vocabulary & Idioms

flying saucer	*n.*	an unknown flying object
		Ex. We were afraid that the flying saucers would land and aliens would come out of them.
defy	*v.*	to challenge
		Ex. The prince chose to defy the king's orders.
saucer	*n.*	a small round shallow dish used to hold a cup
		Ex. The maid served the tea inside teacups with saucers.
globe	*n.*	a spherical body
		Ex. The earth is in the shape of a globe.
multitude	*n.*	a large number
		Ex. There was a multitude of ants on the back porch.
engage	*v.*	to bring troops into conflict or enter into conflict with
		Ex. The two countries engaged in war.
aerial	*adj.*	of, in, or produced by the air
		Ex. The army prepared to launch an aerial assault on the enemy base.
eyewitness	*n.*	a person who actually sees some act, occurrence, or thing firsthand
		Ex. We need an eyewitness of the crime to testify in court.
numerous	*adj.*	many
		Ex. There are numerous ways to complete the task.
radar	*n.*	a device that measures the location of an object by using radio waves
		Ex. All modern aircraft are equipped with radar.
incident	*n.*	an individual occurrence or event
		Ex. The incident was all too embarrassing.
hoax	*n.*	something intended to deceive
		Ex. The whole act was a hoax.

Writing Task #7

▶ Why do you think people try to lose weight?

Model Response

1. Fill in the blanks using the words in the box:

> afraid   aware   different   enough   everyday   follow   form   not
> instead   message   nature   only   stand   these   when   whether

    _____ days, lots of people are trying to lose weight. Some slender people are also trying to do so _____ they are not overweight at all. Why is that?

    First of all, many people are not strong _____ to resist peer pressure. When we do not _____ what others do, we are _____ that others will hate us. This is a _____ of peer pressure. In fact, it is very difficult for us to be strong enough to _____ on our two feet.

    Second, the mass media gives us a false _____ about beautiful people. On television, we usually see young and slender people _____ of old and overweight people. And we believe that _____ young and slender people are beautiful. But what matters is not their looks, but their _____ behavior. Truly beautiful people are people who do good things, _____ people who look good. But the mass media are not _____ of this simple fact and tries to deceive us.

    Finally, we have lost touch with nature. In the world of _____, we are just who we are. We do not try to become _____. But we have lost touch with nature and do not know who we really are.

    For these three reasons, people are trying to lose weight _____ they are really overweight or not.

2. Using your own words, answer the question above. Write your answer on a separate sheet of paper.

Vocabulary & Idioms

space
n. space beyond the atmosphere of the earth
Ex. We could see many stars in space.

rivalry
n. competition
Ex. There was a rivalry between the two schools.

superior
adj. of higher grade or quality
Ex. The company strived to make superior products.

satellite
n. a device launched into orbit around the earth, another planet, the sun, etc.
Ex. We have access to pictures of the earth from our satellites.

insecurity
n. the state of being subject to danger, uncertainty
Ex. With no army, the country was in a state of insecurity.

spur
v. to stimulate
Ex. The carriage driver spurred the horses on with a whip.

bill
n. a proposed law
Ex. Congress wrote a bill to increase taxes.

public relations
actions to promote goodwill with oneself and the public, the community, employees, customers, etc.
Ex. To improve public relations, the company made numerous advertisements.

fruit fly
n. a tiny fly that feeds on the fruit of various plants
Ex. We kept fruit flies in a jar.

fantastic
adj. imaginary, foolish, irrational
Ex. That statement is fantastic.

feat
n. a extraordinary act or achievement
Ex. Eating ten pies was quite a feat.

mankind
n. all humans
Ex. We have made many accomplishments in the history of mankind.

Speaking Task #8

▶ Some children want robots to help them do everyday chores. Others prefer to do housework for themselves. Which do you think is better for children and why?

Model Response

1. Fill in the blanks using the words in the box:

> by   doing   help   importance   lesson   order   steps   truth   waste

In my opinion, doing housework without the _____ of robots is much better for children. First of all, they need to realize the _____ of doing work for themselves. Some people say that doing everyday chores like cleaning is a _____ of time. They are wrong. By doing those things, children become aware that they can do important things _____ themselves. Second, _____ everyday chores teaches children many things about life. By doing those small things, children find out that in _____ to succeed, they need to take a lot of small _____. In fact, this is the most important _____ that children need to learn and doing everyday chores without any help will make them realize this _____.

2. Using your own words, answer the question above. Then talk to the class.

Speak Clearly

3. Complete the sentences choosing the right answer from the box below:

> • work really hard
> • do many things easily

(a) Robots can help people _____.

(b) You must _____ to succeed.

unit 16 Queen Victoria

 Vocabulary & Idioms

reigning	*adj.*	exercising power or authority
		Ex. I am the reigning king of the country.
monarch	*n.*	a king or queen
		Ex. She was the most powerful monarch.
undisputed	*adj.*	agreed upon
		Ex. The explanation was undisputed.
foremost	*adj.*	first in rank, time, or place
		Ex. The foremost surgeons operated at the hospital.
global	*adj.*	referring to the world
		Ex. The professor taught global economics.
ascend	*n.*	to rise
		Ex. The airplane ascended into the air.
heiress presumptive		a female who is expected to be the heir but whose expectations can be canceled by the birth of a closer heir
		Ex. Because the king had no sons, his nephew became heiress presumptive.
heart attack	*n.*	a sudden interruption of the supply of blood to the heart
		Ex. He died of a heart attack.
romance	*n.*	a love affair
		Ex. The couple enjoyed romance during their early years.
propose	*v.*	to make an offer for marriage
		Ex. The man proposed to his girlfriend on a beautiful evening.
companion	*n.*	a domestic partner
		Ex. My dog is my companion.
widow	*n.*	a woman who has lost her husband by death and has not remarried
		Ex. She has been a widow for many years.

Writing Task #8

▸ Why do you think people want to travel to space?

Model Response

1. Fill in the blanks using the words in the box:

> adventures   although   another   everything   explains   including
> opinion   sense   short   take   terrible   who   work   worried

In my _____, there are three kinds of people who want to travel to space. And that _____ why people want to travel to the universe.

First, there are people who have a strong _____ of adventure. They just love _____. They want to experience new things, _____ they might be dangerous. As you may know, we do not know _____ about the universe. So there may be danger in outer space. But adventurous people _____ a risk and travel to space.

Second, there are people who are _____ about our future. Every day we are polluting the earth in many ways and it won't be able to _____ at all. When this happens, we will need to find _____ place where we can live well. The universe may be that kind of place. So we need to travel to space before that _____ thing happens.

Third, there are people who want to know _____ they really are. They believe that they can find the answers in the universe. This is mainly because all of us, _____ the sun and the moon, are connected with the universe. So if we can find out more about it, we may get to know who we really are.

In _____, different people have different ideas about space travel, and the three kinds of people explain to us why people want to travel to space.

2. Using your own words, answer the question above. Write your answer on a separate sheet of paper.

Vocabulary & Idioms

excel
v. to do extremely well in some area
Ex. He excelled at math.

originality
n. creative ability
Ex. Her originality showed in her music.

intimidating
adj. discouraging through fear
Ex. The bull's eyes were intimidating.

adversity
n. a state of hardship or affliction; misfortune
Ex. The football player faced much adversity in his career.

physician
n. a family doctor
Ex. The physician wrote down a prescription for the illness.

tomboy
n. a girl whose behavior is considered to be more like a boy's
Ex. Sue is literally a tomboy.

intervene
v. to interfere, to get involved
Ex. The fight continued until the teacher finally intervened.

botany
n. the study of plants
Ex. I am attending botany class.

seminar
n. a course or subject of study for advanced graduate students
Ex. There is a seminar this afternoon on political science.

genetics
n. the study of heredity or the passing of genes from parents to their young
Ex. The professor teaches genetics at the university.

colleague
n. an associate that one works with
Ex. It is customary to eat lunch with colleagues at the company.

maize
n. corn
Ex. We're having maize for dinner.

Speaking Task #9

▶ If you could have any part-time job, what would it be? Tell us why.

Model Response

1. Fill in the blanks using the words in the box:

> | dream | fascinated | fascinating | greatest | hard |
> |-------|-----------|-------------|----------|------|
> | how | in | laugh | move | telling |

My _____ part-time job is a storyteller. You see, stories have always _____ me and I want to make my listeners fascinated by them. My stories will make my listeners smile, _____, and cry. This is possible because I believe _____ the power of stories and I know _____ to use it wisely. To use the power of stories wisely, you need to tell the truth because only the truth can _____ your listeners. Even if your stories have a lot of _____ elements, you won't be able to fascinate others without _____ them the truth. I have learned this lesson the _____ way and now I believe in the beauty of the truth, which will make me one of the _____ storytellers in the world.

2. Using your own words, answer the question above. Then talk to the class.

Speak Clearly

3. Complete the sentences choosing the right answer from the box below:

> • cry
> • fascinated me

(a) English has always _____.

(b) Sad stories will make you _____.

unit 18 Rocks

 Vocabulary & Idioms

crust
n. the outer layer of something, the external coating
Ex. *The crust was hard and thick.*

erupt
v. to burst forth
Ex. *The volcano erupted.*

subcategory
n. a category within a larger category
Ex. *This subcategory of fish have special characteristics.*

texture
n. the visual and feel of a surface
Ex. *The bread has a very soft texture.*

composition
n. how a substance is formed, what something is made of
Ex. *The composition of the earth is very diverse.*

grain
n. any small hard particle such as sand, gold, pepper, etc.
Ex. *There was no food in the house, not even a grain of rice.*

landscape
n. rural scenery that can be seen from a viewpoint
Ex. *The beautiful landscape was calm and serene.*

cement
v. to bind or join as if with cement
Ex. *The two cemented their relationship.*

evaporate
v. to turn into a gas
Ex. *The water evaporated into the air.*

seasonal
adj. of or dependent on a particular season
Ex. *These flowers are seasonal.*

seafloor
n. the bottom of the ocean
Ex. *The seafloor was filled with coral.*

accumulation
n. the gathering or piling up of something
Ex. *Your accumulation of money has grown quite a bit.*

Writing #9

▶ What is your favorite song? Tell us about it.

Model Response

1. Fill in the blanks using the words in the box:

> appeal   aware   awesome   burst   by   comforting
> come   else   connected   expressive   thin   lyrics
> plot   ready   respect   seems   largely

My favorite song is "You Light Up My Life" _____ Debby Boone. I cannot count how many times I have listened to this _____ song. Whenever I listen to it, I feel _____ to someone with a warm heart.

The _____ of this song can be summarized like this. The character in the song _____ to be a singer who feels lonely and has no hope for the future. So she waits for someone with a kind heart. Then he has _____ and now she is happy. More than anything _____, he gives her hope "to carry on."

That is an _____ story. In addition, Boone has a sweet and _____ voice. When I hear her sing this beautiful song, I always _____ into tears. This is _____ because I feel as if she were the character in the song. Her _____ as a singer is so strong that I feel as if I were in a totally different world.

The words used in the song's _____ are so simple, but touching. In this sense, this is a song for ordinary people who are _____ to meet a person with a sensitive heart. This song also reminds us that we need someone who stands by us through thick and _____.

In short, I love this song because it makes us _____ of truly important things in our lives. In this _____, this song "lights up my life."

2. Using your own words, answer the question above. Write your answer on a separate sheet of paper.

Vocabulary & Idioms

plain
n. a large stretch of level land
Ex. Buffalo roam the plains of America.

devastating
adj. highly destructive
Ex. The tax decision was devastating to the country's economy.

prosperous
adj. wealthy, successful, having good financial fortune
Ex. He made a prosperous business off of selling oranges.

crop rotation
n. the planting of different crops at different times on the same ground in order to avoid depleting the soil
Ex. The farmer would plant corn some years and wheat others to practice crop rotation.

vulnerable
adj. unprotected
Ex. Without his shield, the knight felt very vulnerable.

erosion
n. the wearing away of land by water, glaciers, wind, etc.
Ex. The erosion of the mountains happened over many years.

drought
n. a period of dry weather with no rain
Ex. A drought occurred and crops began to die.

topsoil
n. the fertile upper part of the soil
Ex. The land has good topsoil for planting crops.

barren
adj. infertile, unproductive
Ex. The land was dry and barren.

restore
v. to bring back to former condition
Ex. We must restore the old buildings.

migration
n. when people or animals go from one country, region, etc. to another
Ex. The migration of these birds occurs every fall and spring.

displace
v. to force a person to leave home
Ex. The war displaced many people from their homes.

Speaking Task #10

▶ Some students think that it is OK to copy words from others. Others believe that you should write in your own words. Which do you think is better for students and why?

Model Response

1. Fill in the blanks using the words in the box:

> based   feel   follow   good   grades
> opinion   practice   which   without

In my _____, writing in your own words is much better for students. First of all, if you copy words from others _____ their permission, you will be punished. These days, a lot of people are aware of copyright laws, and students need to _____ those laws. By copying words from others, some students might get good _____, but breaking the law will make them _____ guilty all the time. Second, in order to write well, students need to _____ writing for themselves. Just copying words from others will not make them _____ writers. _____ on their own ideas and experiences, students should try to write in their own words, _____ is the only way to become a good writer.

2. Using your own words, answer the question above. Then talk to the class.

Speak Clearly

3. Complete the sentences choosing the right answer from the box below:

> • hard and lonely
> • be fun
> • trying to write in your own words

(a) Only by _____ can you become a good writer

(b) According to William Zinsser, writing is _____.

(c) In fact, writing can _____.

 **Vocabulary & Idioms**

doctorate
n. one of the highest degrees offered by a university
Ex. *He earned a doctorate at Cornell University.*

professor
n. a teacher of the highest academic rank at a college or university
Ex. *My math professor is Russian.*

beverage
n. a drink
Ex. *What kind of beverages does the restaurant have?*

spoilage
n. the decay of foodstuffs due to the action of bacteria
Ex. *The spoilage of the meat was a pity.*

spontaneously
adv. growing without cultivation or human labor
Ex. *The bacteria seemed to grow spontaneously.*

generate
v. to bring into existence
Ex. *The students generated a long discussion.*

theory
n. an idea or explanation that has not yet been proven
Ex. *The theory that the earth was flat was proven false.*

contamination
n. the act of making impure or unclean
Ex. *The contamination of the water made it harmful to drink.*

cholera
n. an acute intestinal infection caused by the drinking of contaminated water
Ex. *He contracted cholera from drinking the water.*

immune
adj. protected against a disease
Ex. *The shots made him immune to several diseases.*

vaccinate
v. to protect a person from a disease by giving a weakened or killed pathogen, or vaccine to stimulate the production of antibodies in the person's body
Ex. *The doctor vaccinated the patient against smallpox.*

artificially
adv. not according to nature
Ex. *This structure was artificially formed.*

Writing Task #10

▸ Why do you think movies are so popular among people?

Model Response

1. Fill in the blanks using the words in the box:

> analyzing   enjoy   blind   concerns   effective   relieve
> influence   insights   particular   attempts   reflect
> opportunities   fascinated   furthermore

So many people are _____ by movies, and there may be many reasons for that. We can explore those reasons by _____ the needs of people who go to the movies.

First of all, most people need to _____ themselves, and watching movies is one of the most _____ ways to do that. In fact, watching movies helps people to _____ stress coming from everyday life, thus enabling them to have a good time. When people watch movies, they do not have to worry about everyday _____. _____, most movies are great fun.

Second, some people, especially young people, watch movies because they give them good _____ to make friends with other people. As a matter of fact, many young people need to watch movies as part of a _____ date. Such events give young people chances to find out more about each other.

Finally, a large number of people watch movies in order to understand other people and cultures better. This is mainly because most movies are _____ to explore humanity and culture. By watching many different kinds of movies, people come to explore the essence of humanity, which will give them deeper _____ into the human race. In _____, foreign movies get us to explore similarities and differences between various cultures.

In short, different people have different reasons for watching movies. People go to a movie to have fun, to make friends with others, or to _____ on human nature and culture. Movies will continue to _____ us in many ways.

2. Using your own words, answer the question above. Write your answer on a separate sheet of paper.

Memo

Memo

New **Strategic**
Reading Level **3**